What if daydreams are doorways to a higher consciousness?

Angels Whisper to Us
Decoding the Messages in Daydreams

Daria Justyn

Foreword by Psychic Medium Lydia Clar

iUniverse, Inc.
New York Bloomington

Angels Whisper to Us

Decoding the Messages in Daydreams

Copyright © 2008 by Daria Justyn

All rights reserved. No part of this book may be used or reproduced by any means, graphic, electronic, or mechanical, including photocopying, recording, taping or by any information storage retrieval system without the written permission of the publisher except in the case of brief quotations embodied in critical articles and reviews.

The views expressed in this work are solely those of the author and do not necessarily reflect the views of the publisher, and the publisher hereby disclaims any responsibility for them.

iUniverse books may be ordered through booksellers or by contacting:

iUniverse
1663 Liberty Drive
Bloomington, IN 47403
www.iuniverse.com
1-800-Authors (1-800-288-4677)

Because of the dynamic nature of the Internet, any Web addresses or links contained in this book may have changed since publication and may no longer be valid. The views expressed in this work are solely those of the author and do not necessarily reflect the views of the publisher, and the publisher hereby disclaims any responsibility for them.

ISBN: 978-1-4401-0928-7 (pbk)
ISBN: 978-1-4401-0929-4 (ebk)

Printed in the United States of America

iUniverse rev. date: 11/15/2008

~ For my children ~

Chelsea, Jenna & Evan

Anything is possible if it comes from the heart.

Contents

FOREWARD..ix
ACKNOWLEDGMENTS..............................xi
INTRODUCTION....................................xiii
PROLOGUE..xix

Chapter 1
ANGELS SPEAK TO US IN DAYDREAMS...............1

Chapter 2
OUR LOVED ONES COME TO US.......................5

Chapter 3
SIGNS AND WHISPERS.............................11

Chapter 4
ENCOURAGEMENT FROM ABOVE....................19

Chapter 5
CLOUD DANCING...................................27

Chapter 6
PERCHANCE TO DREAM.............................33

Chapter 7
SOMETHING LOST, SOMETHING FOUND...............41

Chapter 8
FORGET ME NOT...................................49

Chapter 9
A MATCH MADE IN HEAVEN.........................57

Chapter 10
FIREWORKS OR FIREFLIES..........................63

Chapter 11
IMAGINARY FRIENDS..............................71

Chapter 12
PURR--FECT SOULS................................77

Chapter 13
SYNCHRONICITY............................83

Chapter 14
CELESTIAL CIRCLES.........................89

Chapter 15
WHEN YOUR MIND GOES ELSEWHERE...............93

Chapter 16
THE LANGUAGE OF DAYDREAMS 99

Chapter 17
DREAMSCAPES 105

Chapter 18
THE CHAKRAS...........................111

Chapter 19
CHAKRA MEDITATION......................119

Conclusion
REVERIE................................123

Daydream Journal 127

FOREWARD

Daria Justyn has gone through the entire developmental process—from beginning to present—because there is no end to knowledge and learning, and has succeeded in becoming the "Great Daydreamer and Phenomenal Communicator."

"Angels Whisper to Us" is testimony to her enormous willpower to succeed while at the same time encouraging others to learn the mental language of Spirit.

This book is just the beginning and I wish her continued success.

Lydia Clar
Psychic Medium

ACKNOWLEDGMENTS

*Feeling gratitude and not expressing it
is like wrapping a present and not giving it.*

~ William Arthur Ward

I am part of a large, loving family, the kind that stories are written about. We laugh, we cry, argue and commiserate, but in the end we always band together. I am blessed to still have both parents in my life, having just celebrated their 60th wedding anniversary, as well as two sisters, two brothers, and their wonderful husbands, wives and children, who are more like my own, than nieces and nephews. We have always been intrinsically connected and have never needed phones to communicate. In fact, the best way to spread news in my family is to use the words, "Don't tell anyone!" I guarantee you by dinner everyone will know. An especially big thank you goes out to my brother, Mark Di Martini, for editing this book—I am so lucky to have a brother who is also an editor—to my son-in-law Ian for dropping everything when I needed your computer expertise, and to Nancy Graham for your well-remembered secretarial skills.

My children have had a challenging life, including a mother who speaks to the dead. But they know we share a special bond, as souls who have chosen to experience this life together, a life that now includes two sons–in–law who are not only accepting of this unusual life style, but loving as well.

Fortune also has smiled on me with an array of extended family members and steadfast friends who could have called me crazy and moved on, but are still by my side and always willing to help—you know who you are.

To each of you, please know that everything else pales in comparison to how blessed I feel to have all of you in my life. I'll love you forever.

I'd also like to extend a special thank you to Lydia Clar. Meeting her was one of those rare, indisputably life-changing moments when dreams and destiny collide.

I first read about her psychic gifts in medium John Edward's book, and in speaking with her realized we had unknowingly spent years at opposite ends of the same Jersey City street. That was the beginning of an extraordinary relationship.

Our initial meeting was a revelation. When I sat down in front of her, she looked me in the eye and said, "You have a gift and you're not using it!" I knew exactly what she meant and I even remember my reply: "Every time I try I feel like they're closing the door." Of course at the time I wasn't sure who "they" were, but not to worry, Lydia knew.

Since then our lives have become powerfully intertwined. She became my mentor and friend, guiding me along on this ever-expanding journey. We discovered that her grandfather and my great-grandfather were both born on the Spanish island of Majorca. Not a small coincidence, if you believe in those, which I don't. I often wonder what else lies hidden in our past, waiting to be uncovered. But one thing I do understand is why she came into my life. One night, my guides revealed to me that Lydia had been "put in place in my life to assist me" in delivering this most important message: *that daydreams are tools for spiritual awareness and soul development.* I thank you, Lydia, for sharing your wisdom, your heart, and for always being just a phone call away.

INTRODUCTION

*Those who dream by day are cognizant of many things
which escape those who dream only by night.*

- Edgar Allan Poe

All of humanity daydreams. It is a gift we all share. Call it a fantasy, a reverie, a vision, an altered state, it doesn't matter. We all have experienced it. There exists a commonality about daydreams that poet Robert Browning expresses so beautifully when he writes about being "stung by the splendor of sudden thought." In every culture, despite all of our differences, we all daydream.

I have written *Angels Whisper to Us* because I passionately believe that *daydreams are doorways to a higher consciousness.* They deliver messages through which we receive guidance, inspiration and acknowledgement, that come to us from our Angels, spirit guides and loved ones who have passed on, and are a direct link to our soul. I like to think of the soul as a reflection of God, therefore these messages, regardless of how they are delivered, come from a higher source.

On a clear, sunny day, I received a message from the Archangels. It came in the form of a voice whispering that filled every fiber of my being with a "knowing" that daydreams are a doorway to a higher consciousness, a bridge between the physical and spiritual world.

But my writing didn't start out that way. I clearly remember typing away about my life as a psychic medium, growing up with a mother who saw dead relatives, when I heard a voice say: "Angels whisper to us in daydreams." Let me clarify that: it was more like hearing it as a voice that sounded very different from my own, and seeing it in my mind at the same time. It came as an inspirational thought magnified a thousand times over. But it also came as a vibration which nearly knocked me off my chair, accompanied by waves of goose bumps that caused me to stop. I felt completely humbled. I guess my Angels and spirit guides had a different plan for me then I had for myself.

I have always had an intimate relationship with Angels from the time I was a little girl, sensing them in my room and praying for them to protect me. Since then, I've been receptive to the energies of Archangel Gabriel, Michael, Uriel and Raphael and have, over the years, worked to develop a clear communication through meditation. Yet this message was an instant revelation for me. As a child who was repeatedly told by teachers to stop daydreaming and pay attention, I finally felt vindicated.

That was the beginning of an ongoing journey. I began to question what actually happens when we daydream. I looked at *when it happens* [anytime], *where it happens* [anywhere] and *how it happens* [through no effort on our part]. How could this be? Why would this seemingly magical ability to daydream so effortlessly be given to us, and what was its function in our life and for our soul? Was it a connection or continuation of our night dreams, or was it something entirely separate?

One thing I learned for certain while composing this book, and I use the word composing because I felt like an instrument in the hands of the Archangels, is that if you ask the questions, you will receive the answers. It will usually come to you in a daydream, as an inspired thought, when you are least expecting it.

So if we are inspired through daydreams, where does this inspiration actually come from? Everyone speaks about being inspired, but I took this one step further and it actually made perfect sense to me.

As a psychic medium I am always asked this question: "How can you tell the difference between what is real and what is imagined?" I tell them that there is no difference. The things we imagine are just as authentic as the things we hold in our hand. We believe that in order for something to be real we have to be able to touch it. But nothing is really solid, that concept is just an illusion as molecules are always in motion. Most of us grow up believing the same thing about daydreams and imagination because we've been conditioned to do so.

Let's examine imagination. When we imagine, we visualize something in our mind; the possibilities are infinite. However this imagining is the beginning of the creative process that actually takes something intangible, and manifests it into reality. The advent of quantum physics has thrown loopholes into many long-standing scientific theories. It has been discovered that there are things in this universe that do not appear until you look for them. It is the actual energy of focusing on them that seemingly pulls them out of nowhere. Imagine you are gazing up at the night sky and seeing it completely black, void of stars and other heavenly bodies. You question, "Where are all the stars?" Then you begin to really focus your attention on the sky, and as if on cue, all the stars and planets begin to appear.

This concept blew my mind, but when I equate that with what happens when we daydream, that through daydreams we are *inspired*, then we *imagine*, and then we *create*, it resonates as logical, beautiful and true.

I now recognize what the Archangels were helping me to understand, like some secret, hidden away until humanity was ready for it to be revealed: that daydreams are the vehicle, the doorway through which this inspiration and information comes to us. With their celestial guidance, I have come to believe that this message is for every man and woman on the planet, and should be taught to our children from birth. This process transcends barriers of race, religion and culture. It replaces *fear* with *faith*, and empowers us to trust our intuition. It shows us the necessity of releasing antiquated, control-based beliefs that create confusion and insecurity.

This concept of the power of daydreams is so intrinsically simple, how could it not be true? Like the rest of the universe, the deeper you look, the simpler it becomes. When you fall into that state of what seems like suspended animation, a door is opened. You are able to receive messages from a higher vibrational source, and then you are returned to the present moment. You need only to learn how to pay attention to it.

Writing this manuscript has been a metaphysical experience. I remember writing the words, and seeing them appear on the page, but they seemed to be coming from a place outside of myself. When I would go back and review a page, I thought, "Did I really write that?" But I understood that the messages coming through me, from what I believe is a Council of Angels, flowed from my hands and onto the page. I knew, without a shadow of a doubt, that my faith and trust in this hierarchy allowed the process to happen. Imagine my surprise when I realized how beautifully simple and uncomplicated this idea about daydreaming really is. *Daydreams create an awakening.* They remind us that within us lies the power to manifest whatever we need to accomplish our soul's mission here on Earth.

Next was the monumental task of presenting this extremely unusual idea to the public. I wondered if it would be met with criticism or incredulity. I began to introduce the idea during readings and was delighted with the response: *every single person* who listened to this idea responded with a positive curiosity; they just never thought about daydreams in that way before. They never really examined their daydreams, or the reason why they daydream at all. It was just something that everyone did, like breathing. But they were ready to listen.

Why me, why am I the daydream emissary? I ask myself that question all the time. As a young child I always felt a really strong connection with Angels. They were my guardians, heavenly beings sent to watch over me, standing like sentinels, ready to fight off the demons in my nightmares. Perhaps they prepared me for this role by guiding me as a medium, to be a messenger for others. Or maybe because I have always felt there was something I was supposed to do with my life that was different or unconventional and continually sought that out. "Ask and you shall receive."

This is my life's purpose. I know that now. I challenge you to ask the questions and the answers will be given to you.

So that is how this book evolved. I have written it from my perspective, using my stories and experiences as a psychic medium, but I do want to emphasize, that you do not need to be psychic or a medium, to understand and benefit from the information in this book. I know this to be true because when I do a reading it's like having a daydream. The only difference is that the information coming through is for someone other than me. I ask you to read this book with an open mind and heart, and to:

- TRUST that every daydream is a vibrational connection to your soul, sending messages and inspiration from guardian Angels, spirit guides and loved ones. If you do, it will give you real, tangible help to fulfill your soul's mission in this life.

- BELIEVE that what comes to you comes for a reason and with a purpose, and if you pay attention it will help you attract what you need into your life.

- ACT upon the messages that come in daydreams and know that you have opened a door filled with guidance, inspiration, acknowledgement, and love. *You can do this.*

As philosopher John Locke wrote in 1699: *"The thoughts that come often unsought, and, as it were, drop into the mind, are commonly the most valuable of any we have."* So go ahead, open the daydream door.

With love and gratitude,
Daria Justyn

PROLOGUE

If the mind is open and awake...
then do the gods partake to fill the spaces in between
the dreamer and his dream.

~ Sarah Pere

You slowly drift off. There is a moment of surrender, and then you are suddenly flooded with sights and sounds. A name, a place, an event comes to you in an instant, then you are jolted back to your surroundings with the recognition that you were given the answer to a question; one that has been lingering in the back of your mind. It is as if you have been given the piece to a puzzle that fits into place.

Consider this metaphor: think of all the creatures that live in our oceans. Their world exists under the water, and although there is another world above them, vast universes in fact, they get glimpses of it only if they break the surface of the water, and only for a moment. As the tide washes over the starfish settling into a tide pool, the dolphin spinning up through the surf toward the sun, or the whale rising to gather plankton before slamming back down through the waves, there is a moment of awakening where they feel the sun and the air before returning to the great blue.

For us, daydreaming offers the same brief grasp of lucidity; sticking your head above the water and observing all you can, before you have to duck under again.

We live in a time when everything seems to happen at warp speed. Life is so rushed, so crazy, it is no surprise that we have all but shut down our capacity to relax and daydream. This was not always the way. In many cultures daydreaming was, and still is, considered a sacred experience. The "vision quest" initiated by Native Americans, or the "walkabout" embarked upon by the Aborigines of New Zealand and Australia could very well have been initiated by daydreams. And what of the ancient civilizations and their modern counterparts who use hallucinogenic plants in ceremonies to induce the trance-like state of daydreaming? Are they trying to re-create those elusive moments that come to us when we daydream?

Whenever you pause, lost in thought, whenever you fall into that dreamy state of reflection, you open a doorway, a portal, and the opportunity to connect to that "other place" where souls reside. In this place of daydreams exists all that was, and all of eternity. This is the place our souls come from and ultimately return home to. Embracing the power of daydreams and where they come from, brings us closer to understanding the true meaning of our Earthly mission and *why we are here*. By learning to *decode the messages in daydreams*, you can begin to use them as tools to attract what ever your soul needs to experience here on Earth. Daydreams are the key to unlocking that door.

Chapter 1

ANGELS SPEAK TO US IN DAYDREAMS

The angels are so enamored of the language that is spoken in heaven that they will not distract their lips with the hissing and unmusical dialects of men, but speak their own, whether there be any who understand it or not.
~ Ralph Waldo Emerson.

Do you ever think about where daydreams come from? They light upon us like butterflies, landing at a moment when we are least expecting them. They come to us at the most unusual times; when we are eating, showering, doing chores, talking a walk, usually relaxed. But daydreams always come out of the blue, and have you ever stopped to think about why we "dream while we are awake?"

Angels speak to us in daydreams. They whisper in our ear when our mind is quiet of all the responsibilities and cares that we carry with us each day. When the voice in our head running down the list of what needs to be done, or picked up, or paid for is finally silenced, if only for a few moments. Daydreams are the pathway for our loved ones on the other side to give us that nudge we need to let us know we are not alone. They open a space for our intuition to "phone home" and connect with our soul, keeping us on the right path.

We come into this life with a plan, events charted throughout our lives. As each challenge comes up, snippets of helpful guidance come to us through our daydreams. They let us slip into that beautiful state of reverie that allows our Angels and spirit guides to bestow what I call "little gems" upon us.

It was through a near collision that I first made the connection that the message that probably saved my life came in a daydream. As often as I try not to daydream while I'm driving we all know it happens. How often have you been driving, daydreaming, when out of nowhere you hear a voice in your head telling you to slow down, or you just instinctively know to turn direction, or stop? And by doing so you averted a dangerous situation?

I remember a time I was driving on the Garden State Parkway in New Jersey with my three young children in the car. There was only one other car in sight, up ahead and directly in front of us. I knew I was daydreaming when I was startled by a voice that whispered in my ear, as clearly as if they were standing next to me, saying "Slow down!"

My eyes went right to the speedometer. I wasn't speeding but I stepped on the brake anyway. Just at that moment, the car in front of us spun out of control, managed to get turned around, and was coming straight at us.

I felt that what happened next was surreal, like it was all moving in slow motion. I glanced to my left, and saw the driveway for the State Police station. It seemed to appear out of nowhere. I turned the wheel in that direction, and slid into the parking lot, skidding to a stop, unharmed. The driver of the other car had turned a complete circle, glanced over at me, and sped away. I turned to my children, making sure they were all right, and then burst into tears, thanking my Guardian Angels, the Blessed Mother, and anyone else I could think of that might have spoken to me. If I had not have heard that voice in my ear and acted upon it, the outcome might have been very different.

I always make a conscious effort not to daydream while I'm driving or doing something equally as dangerous. Common sense takes precedence here, to remain alert when you need to be. But if you do slip into a daydream at an inappropriate moment, be thankful that your Angels and spirit guides have a way of jumping in and using it as a way of protecting you by saying, "Snap out of it!"

They will utilize your daydream to startle you into action. You don't have to stop to think about the message coming through, who it is coming from or ponder what it means. It is definitive for the moment, and gets you to react instantaneously.

If I were having a conversation would I have heard the voice? I don't think so. But we can't spend our lives in silence. Instead we learn to trust, knowing that the doorway of the daydream is there, available for our soul, to get us the help we need at the moment we need it.

Can we be saved from every single dangerous situation that comes our way? No, because then we would be prevented from experiencing the challenges that our souls are meant to take on in this lifetime. But this is where faith comes in; believing that our Angels, spirit guides and our loved ones who have crossed over will all be there to step in when we most need their guidance.

For me, this daydream became a moment of grace, when I was given a gift, the gift of awareness, and I paid attention.

Chapter 2

OUR LOVED ONES COME TO US

Come to me darling; I'm lonely without thee;
daytime and nighttime I'm dreaming about thee.

~ Samuel Taylor Coleridge

Our loved ones come to us in daydreams. We experience them as a snapshot in our mind, as a fragrance that lingers for an instant, or a feeling evoked from a memory of past times.

Have you ever seen or heard something that reminds you of a loved one who has passed on? You hear a tune on the radio, or you go past a sign with their name it. Suddenly you slip into a daydream and there they are. For a moment in time, you are with them again. You see them, but not in a place that is familiar to you. You feel as if they are trying to show you an image, but it is just out of reach. Something distracts you, and you realize you have finished a task with no recollection of having done so. When you recall the images, you question what it is they were trying to show you. This is usually the moment when your mind moves into distrust; choosing to believe the daydream was merely a mental trick, instead of a revelation.

Loved ones come to acknowledge their presence in your life. It is their way of letting you know you are not alone, that you have help from the other side, even years after their passing. Whether you are grieving, or reliving happy memories, they will do their best to come to you in daydreams. They will find ways to validate their presence through your daydreams, by giving you some kind of sign, something to remind you of them.

Deceased family and friends often come to us while we are sleeping. So often I hear my clients say they dreamt of a loved one, and they didn't know whether or not it was real. It is the same for daydreams; people will tell me they were daydreaming of someone and could I tell them if that person was trying to come through to them. The answer is *yes, yes, yes*! Those who have crossed over will often come to you in your dreams, while you are sleeping. When you doubt that, they will enter your daydreams as if to say, "OK, you didn't believe it was me in your dream, but you are wide awake now and here I am again."

That daydream was their opportunity to send you a message. Are you going to pay attention, or will you say it isn't possible?

This story is very special to me. It was the first time that I was able to connect a stranger who came to me in a daydream as "belonging" to someone else. It was a validation for me that all the people who had been wandering around in my daydreams were souls who had real, live family members waiting to hear from them. It was the experience that really brought home the fact that my mission in life was to deliver these messages to whoever was supposed to be on the receiving end. It really was as simple as that; as simple as having a daydream, and learning to become interactive with it. Well maybe not so simple in the beginning because I wanted to just run up to everyone I thought I had a message for. I learned from psychic medium Lydia Clar, my mentor extraordinaire, that if I was supposed to give someone a message, I would have to trust that they would be put in my path. Not everyone is ready. So one afternoon, while I was sitting having a cup of tea, I had this daydream: A handsome, dark-haired man jumped down from the back of a delivery truck. He wore a gray zippered jacket, the kind that was part of a uniform, and he was holding an oxygen mask in his hand. Behind him, the floor of the truck was scattered with ice cream and snacks, and I noticed an open can of coffee. The ringing of a phone startled me, and I realized I had been deep in a daydream. Although it had only been for an instant, the scene was very vivid, and if you think about daydreams, it can seem like a mini movie is shown in your head in the blink of an eye.

Later on in the day I met up with my friend Nancy, to return a ring that was hers. Nancy is the kind of friend that from the moment you meet you know you have a kinship, or soul connection with. She told me she had just come from an antique store. It was during the Christmas holidays, and as she wandered the aisles she found herself daydreaming about Christmas as a little girl, nostalgic for her parents who were both deceased. As she tuned in to the music playing in the background, she recognized the song as a favorite of her late father, Joe. She was drawn toward the back of the store, and there stood a silver Christmas tree, exactly like the one her mother put up every year. Under the tree, was an old ashtray from a restaurant. It said "Joe's Pier 52." Not only was that her dad's name, his birthday was May 2, or 5/2.

So here she was, having been led into a store, where she got to see her mother's favorite tree, while listening to her father's favorite song. It was almost as if her parents were giving her a gift, letting her relive the memory of being together for the holidays. This was quite a moving experience for her.

I don't know why, but as I handed her the ring I felt compelled to tell her about my daydream, and as I did, she began to cry. "That man", she said, "was my father. He drove a truck, delivering ice cream, and wore a gray jacket just like the one you described. When I was a young girl, every Friday night, he and my mom played cards with friends. They wanted to include me, so it was my job to put out the snacks and make the coffee. He died when I was sixteen. He used the oxygen mask as a reference to my mom, Beverly, who passed from lung cancer. This ring was a gift from my father." "So was this daydream," I replied.

What a revelation. You could have knocked me over with a feather. This was a defining moment in my life, where I literally felt destiny touch my soul. The timing was perfect. Nancy's father Joe used my daydream to validate her experience so that she would know, without a shadow of a doubt that her parents would be sharing the holidays with her. The fact that I had her ring helped me to remember, or anchor the daydream, in my memory. For me, sharing this story with Nancy and realizing the implications gave me the courage I needed to start doing readings for others—going public—if you will. This was not so easy for someone who spent many a night with her head under the covers, afraid of ghostly visitors. After that, I learned to focus in on my daydreams and in time, with practice, I could daydream at will.

So what makes my daydreams, or visions different from yours, *nothing*! I have just learned to relax through meditation, and allow myself to go into a space of stillness that just lets the daydreams come to me. Then I am able to discern whether the message is for me, my family or friends, or for someone else. You can do this, too. But your focus should not be on how psychic you can become, but how well you can develop your intuition, be open to inspiration and be receptive to the messages which will, in turn, help you to attract good energy into your life.

Another validation, what I like to call "an illumination of love", came to me through a daydream after a reading I had given to a young man whose mother had passed on. He was a wonderful, joyful person, who seemed exuberant and full of life. He and his wife had been blessed with a daughter, whom they named Rose, after his mom. During our conversation, his mother's soul came through with some strong validations. She wanted him to know she was still with him and his family, and acknowledged their little girl, her namesake. She kept showing me butterflies. I asked him if it might have something to do with his daughter's room, a picture or statuette, but there were no butterflies anywhere. Then, with certainty, I realized it was a symbol, a way his mother could give him a sign. I told him to pay attention.

A few days later I found myself daydreaming and the name Rose popped into my head. I couldn't place it, and tucked it into the recesses of my mind. I knew eventually I would understand, probably sooner then later, because now I knew that my daydreams were vehicles. That same afternoon, I got a phone call. It was the young man for whom I had done the reading. He had gone outside on the porch to sit with members of his family and share the details of his reading. When he got to the part about his mom giving him a sign, a butterfly landed right on his lap! True to her word, his mom had used a butterfly at exactly the right moment, to touch him. Her name was Rose, the name in my daydream. He thanked me and said a teary goodbye.

I think that was the first time I realized how, through daydreams, we are all connected, and how our guides and loved ones on the other side are working really hard to get us all in sync. That way we can have those serendipitous moments we like to call coincidences and why it's a good idea to keep a daydream journal. When you find yourself daydreaming about a specific person or event, make a note of it and the time it happened. You may be surprised to find that someone else you know was being contacted from the other side as well, because, truly, there are no coincidences, only divine intervention.

Chapter 3

SIGNS AND WHISPERS

What could be more mysterious then something comes to us in a daydream.

- Emerson

So much about the afterlife is a mystery. You want to believe, but sometimes you just can't wrap your mind around such abstract ideas as spirits and guides, things you can't see with your own eyes. After all "seeing is believing," isn't it?

But then those strange occurrences happen; the sound not quite there, the feather-like touch, the chills on the back of your neck; experiences you *feel*, not see. And somehow, when you stop to think about it, they seem to happen right after you have been daydreaming. So you ask yourself, "Could this be a soul, a guide, an Angel, someone trying to make contact?" The answer is *absolutely*.

Most of us grow up being taught that the dead and our guardian Angels are "over there" and we are "over here", and as comedians Abbott and Costello used to say, "And never the twain shall meet!" In this age of media-obsessed instant gratification and information at the touch of a button, it's easy for the subtle, energetically-driven signals that come from the other side to get lost in translation. When it comes to dealing with spirits, guides and Angels, we expect to get great big messages and neon signs, instead of fleeting images sent in a flash, and little whispers that leave us wondering. Yet energy can be a powerful tool, a motivational force to get things moving. They absolutely use energy to send us signals, and these signals often come *after* we daydream—a light flickers, a phone rings, a picture falls, a dog barks at nothing, or a feather lands at our feet. These are the kinds of validations that give us something our senses can register. This energy can help us cut through confusion, dissolve doubt and open us up to the possibility of seeing life from a different angle. If you allow yourself to follow it, you might be surprised to find where it will lead.

I grew up in a house where signs were flying left and right. But after thinking about it, I remembered that they usually happened *after* the fact. If the phone rang or someone showed up in conversation, or literally at the door, it was usually after one of us had been daydreaming about them and decided to mention it, and poof, there they were. I believe people often get it wrong when they say they were thinking about someone, when actually they were daydreaming about them. *Their soul was contacting your soul through a daydream.*

Daydreams also connect you to your intuition. "If only I had listened to my intuition" is a phrase everyone has used at one time or another. Think about it: how many times have you decided to do something that didn't feel quite right, but for one reason or another you talked yourself into doing it anyway. You start to get ready, loose yourself in preparation, when out of nowhere a sentence pops into your head that says, "Don't do it!" The reason I say sentence is because signs don't always come as a voice bellowing in your ear. The thought can just appear in your head, or you'll feel it in the pit of your stomach. Daydreams can engage all of your senses, and you can feel things just as much as you can see or hear them.

But if you listened to your intuition, acted upon it, and it resulted in a good outcome, then your daydream did its job of delivering that message and possibly preventing you from making a grave mistake.

I think I was the biggest daydreamer of all time, always being teased by my family and reprimanded at school. When I was a little girl I used to go outside to sit on the porch and daydream. My mom came outside one evening and found me looking up, searching the skies. When she asked what I was daydreaming about, I told her I was waiting for a spaceship to come and get me. She asked if I was afraid, and I said, "Oh no, I'm excited about going, as long as they bring me back." Then she laughed and said, "Well, its supper time, so they'll have to come back later." I must have been one weird kid. But then again, when you have a mother who wakes up saying someone's going to die because she was dreaming of babies, I guess we can say the pear doesn't fall far from the tree. Sorry, mom.

But it wasn't as if in my family, we spent all of our time waiting for apparitions or voices from beyond. It's just that we would get these gentle kinds of acknowledgements—and they came on a regular basis—acknowledgement about friends and relatives, warnings and validations. Looking back, I think we had days where we felt the psychic vibes more then others, where some instances felt kind of special, and we said so, but we never thought about it in terms of psychic phenomenon. Maybe that's the key: when you replace the words *psychic phenomenon* with *daydream phenomenon*, you open up a world of possibilities, a world where everyone can train themselves to be psychic, just by doing something that comes naturally.

There have been times though, when I've tried to tune out my daydreams, spirits and guides included, thinking I didn't need any guidance. We are, after all, responsible for our own soul's journey, and even with guidance we still have to take responsibility for making our own decisions. Yet it never fails to amaze me how often they will help us in spite of ourselves, and how much easier everything flows when we welcome them into our daydreams and our lives.

Messages will come during very emotional times; especially when we're excited and our energy is unusually high, when we are feeling truly blessed and wishing our deceased family and friends were there to celebrate with us.

Guess what: they are! It's easier for them to connect with us through our daydreams and make their presence known when our vibrations are high.

They are also there for us when we are afraid, when our knees are knocking and we feel frozen. Fear can put up a giant wall that gets bigger and bigger and blocks our daydreams, until we decide to break through it. That doesn't mean our Angels and spirit guides aren't ready and waiting. Fear just makes it harder for us to stay open and intercept the guidance that is always available. Think about it: isn't it true that after you have conquered a fear, you feel liberated, experiencing some kind of self-realization or revelation? You have let your guard down and suddenly a path opens up.

There was a time, when I was really coming into my own as a medium, when I felt petrified. I had been repeatedly dreaming about a red-haired woman who was trying to talk to me. Then one night, I woke up and she started to appear right in front of me. It's hard to explain, even now. I felt like I was looking at a fuzzy television screen that was trying to clear itself up. Her image was getting bigger and bigger until I jumped out of bed and she disappeared. I paced the floors and I literally didn't sleep for three nights. That's when I called Lydia, at my wits end, who by this time was mentoring me. She explained that this woman, who was trying to come to me in my dreams, was a guide. By staying frozen in fear, I was blocking her from helping me with my psychic development. Once I understood this, I was able to let go of the fear and embrace the help that I knew was being offered to me. Thank God for Lydia! I had spent so many years being afraid of my ability. This was a major turning point for me.

It also becomes more difficult for us to feel the energy of our guides when we are sad. Our energy is low and the vibrations we emit make it harder for them to reach us. We envelop ourselves in a veil of tears, like a mist that rests over the surface of the water at mornings first light, and they can't get through. Reminiscent of walking in fog, you might hear or feel someone off in the distance, yet you can't find your way to them until the mist clears. But when we are sad we cry and crying can be very cleansing for the soul. It helps us to express and move through our grief. It is equally important to express sadness as it is to express joy. Yet as twilight is balanced by dawn, so must sadness be balanced by joy. Your daydreams will bring you joy. Be open and let them, for your Angels will be waiting patiently, standing guard and always at the ready.

I often find my daydreams being used as vehicles to deliver messages to my friends, because they "on the other side" know I am open for it. *When you daydream you are open.* Here was an instance where I had invited a friend over for lunch, but the soul who showed up before her wasn't exactly the kind of visitor I was expecting.

I have a very dear friend, Fran, whose dad passed on a few years ago. Arthur Kroll was a gentleman, dignified, sweet and cordial, who always had a smile on his face and an interesting story to tell. He lived to be almost 100 years old and accomplished so much during his lifetime. When you live that long you see so many changes in the world. Often I would visit, and listening to him was like opening a window onto a different world.

Fran has a picture of her dad and mom, taken years ago, while they were attending a cocktail party. Arthur looked so handsome and dashing in his white tuxedo. He reminded me of a young Sean Connery, suave and ready for adventure. I was really sorry to see him leave this Earth, but so happy that he passed peacefully at home. We have special threads that connect us: he and my daughter, Chelsea, share the same birthday, and my daughter Jenna, was born on his wedding anniversary.

A few months ago, I called Fran and invited her to come to my house for lunch. Fran is an antique dealer and a gifted artist. Besides that, we share a love for collecting and an enthusiasm for flea markets that would leave you all in the dust. So although we see and speak to each other all the time, it had been a while since she had come to my home.

I was in my kitchen preparing lunch when I started daydreaming about her dad. Like watching a movie, I saw him playing golf, a sport he loved. He had outlived all of his partners. He lived across the street from the golf course, and took pride in the fact that he had his own key to the gate, which was directly opposite his house. Having the key meant a lot to him when he could no longer drive. This meant he wouldn't have to go all the way around to the front entrance, which was an impossibly long walk for him.

I snapped out of my daydream and started rushing around; trying to get lunch in order, when I remembered that I'd promised to look up some information for a client. I stopped what I was doing and went into my bedroom and pulled out the book I needed. When I opened the cover, out fell a funeral card with Arthur Kroll's name on it. You know those cards the family gives you with a prayer or remembrance on it? I can't explain how it got there; I have no memory of putting it there. I could make no connection between this book and his death, and I hadn't picked the book up in months. When Fran arrived, I was able to say with certainty that her father knew she was coming over and would be joining us.

Soon after that, my son, Evan, and I were going on a trip to California to visit my daughter, Chelsea, and her husband, Ian. I was unusually apprehensive about getting on the plane, since this time Evan would be with me. I'm not usually nervous on planes, but with my son on board, vivid memories of childhood flights with my mother chanting the rosary amid lightening flashes and thunder claps were flooding back and the phrase "we're going down, we're going down" kept reverberating in my head.

We took our seats. I pulled out my ever-present rosary beads, and glanced up the aisle to see a man looking back at me, smiling. Astonishingly, it was Mr. Kroll. I did a double take, but he was gone. I was left looking at the back of someone else's head, but his image was clear and vivid in my mind. I immediately calmed down, and knew I had nothing to be fear. I knew it was Arthur's way of reassuring me, letting me know that on our trip he would be watching over us.

As I am writing this story, the phone rings. It is Fran calling to say hello. Mysterious? No. She was just daydreaming about me and decided to call. But I know her dad was whispering in her ear…

When you feel the energy from the other side sailing in on a daydream and arrive as a sweet surprise, even if you aren't sure where it will lead, believe, pay attention, and learn as you go. Whether the change it initiates is small or large, it always creates a ripple effect that touches every part of your life. The energy can be subtle or it can make you feel like a powerful, positive surge swept down from the heavens and scooped you up like the tide rolling in. Be open to it and let the plans your soul has created for you unfold.

Chapter 4

ENCOURAGEMENT FROM ABOVE

*I think we dream so we don't have to be apart so long.
If we're in each others dreams, we can play together all night.*

- Bill Watterson

I was dreaming. It was a crystal clear day, with a sky so blue you had to shield your eyes. I turned and saw that I was talking to my nephew, Matthew. We were in a field of grass that went on forever. His dog, Ruby, who had passed on, was running around our feet, rolling in the wild flowers. I was reminded of a line from "The Wizard of Oz": "We're not in Kansas anymore." I looked up and thought: Matthew has grown, he seems taller. I smiled at him and heard a voice saying, "Matt, it's going to be you, you're going to be the one playing soccer." Then I woke up.

I called my sister, Stephanie, Matthew's mom, to tell her about the dream. I was excited because it was so vivid. She told me Matthew had played a soccer game the day before and won. Another game was played that day, on the same field, after his team had finished. One of the players from that game crashed his car on the way home and was killed. Matt was friendly with the boy's mom, and had spoken to her during the game. Before she even said it, I saw the boy's name in my head. It was unsettling.

Two weeks later, I had a day of readings scheduled at a client's home. That morning, I woke up with a vivid memory of what I had been dreaming. I dreamt I was in someone's house and I was there to do readings. The television was on and it was very noisy. I couldn't concentrate and had to ask everyone to tone it down. One of the people I was supposed to read was named Ronnie, and I was waiting for her to show up. There was also a woman in the house who was the mom. Her name was Marie Kaye, or Marie Kate. When I woke up, I couldn't quite remember which. I just felt very frustrated that something important was supposed to happen and I couldn't remember it.

On the ride over to do the actual readings I started daydreaming, and it all came rushing back. In my head I saw the images and heard the names again from the night before. I decided I would ask each person if these names meant anything to them.

I arrived, greeted my first client, and began. Although we were in a room with the door closed, I had to interrupt my first reading to ask the group to turn off the television and please quiet down, just as I had dreamt. When I got to the fifth person, I could feel the energy in the room shift. The name, "Ronnie", came up. She had a friend by that name, but couldn't make a connection. Later on in the reading, a soul came through who had died in a car accident. It was a young man, he was in high school, and he gave me his name and age. She didn't know him. I then asked her, "Have you spoken to Ronnie lately?" She let out a gasp, as it all came to light. Just the day before, she had been speaking to Ronnie. Ronnie was telling her about a friend whose son had been killed in a car accident. He was in high school and had been driving home from a soccer game. Suddenly, recalling my dream about Matthew, I asked her if she knew what school he was from, and when this happened. She did. This was the same boy who knew Matthew.

I ended the reading and we went out to join the group. She wanted to share this with the rest of the group. During their conversation, I heard the name "Marie Kaye," come up and asked, "What did you just say?" They all looked at me in astonishment. There was the other name from my dream, validating that this woman for whom I had just read, was being visited by this young soul in the hopes of getting his message through, for Ronnie and for his mom, the mom that Matthew had spoken to. How did I know this? She sells products for a company named "Marie Kaye."

The next day I spoke to the woman who'd had the reading. She called to thank me, and validate some more information. It turns out that during the time she was with me, her friend, Ronnie, was visiting with the boy's mom. I'm sure he knew that and took the opportunity to come through. I'm sure the voice I heard in my dream about Matthew was this boy, acknowledging that he knew Matt had spoken to his mother, giving him encouragement about the game they both loved, and why, in my dream, Matt appeared in a large, green field, a perfect soccer field. From his vantage point, this young man was seeing things we couldn't and he used the opportunity to reach out and give some encouragement from above. It's easy for people to say it's a coincidence. I say, please, take the time to appreciate the beautiful, elaborate and intricately- planned sequence of events, arranged from the other side, brought to you courtesy of a daydream. Do you see now why it's so important to pay attention?

But encouragement can come in many different ways. This time, it came in the form of an introduction that manifested itself first in a night dream, and then continued on, from daydream to daydream, weaving a pattern until the message was complete.

In this dream, I was standing in front of a man with sparkling blue eyes named Josh, who introduced himself as my new spirit guide. He had brought along someone very special, who would also act as a guide. She had long, gray wispy hair and wore glasses; so much for every guide having wings and halos!

I remember thinking, "Do I have to pay her? Maybe we can barter." But by the way she was looking at me I knew payment wasn't necessary.

As she came closer to me, everything became suddenly very lucid, and I realized she looked familiar. She had actually already appeared in a dream I'd had, just the night before. In it, I was in a house, surrounded by a group of souls who were there to test my psychic ability. I glanced down the hall and saw two people walk by. They were bright blue and clearly emanating an aura of blue light, and I thought, "That's strange, what's up with the blue people." But my attention was drawn back to my group as I was handed a bracelet, asked to look at it, hold it and identify its owner. I looked around, and saw a young girl standing in front of me. Since it was the type of bracelet she would wear, it was easy to assume it was hers. I shared these thoughts with them, because I wanted to be as honest as possible for something so important. A woman stepped forward to compliment me on my integrity, and said *that* was the true test, and I had passed. This was the same woman with the gray wispy hair that I was now being introduced to as a guide.

When I woke up, I recalled the dream and wondered if it was real—even I have my doubts sometimes. While I was driving to work, I started thinking about this woman who would be a new guide, and wondered what her name was. I soon fell into daydreaming. I always laugh when I think of my nephew Frankie, bursting into the room saying, "Aunt Daria, I was honking my horn at you, hanging out the window yelling, and you still drove right past me with that spaced out look on your face. It amazes me how you get anywhere!"

Anyway, in my daydream, I was hearing snippets of a tune; "Daisy, Daisy, something, something with eyes so blue." I snapped back and remembered that was a song my aunt played on the piano when I was very young. I thought, "Ok, your name is Daisy" but somehow I wasn't really convinced.

Later that evening, I was driving around town, thinking about the Daisy song. Doubt was still creeping in, I needed something more. I called Lydia on my cell phone to tell her about it and how I wasn't convinced, I need a sign. While I was speaking to her, I glanced to my left, and saw a tavern with a sign in front of it, showing the name of the band that was playing. The sign said, "PSYCHO DAISY" in really big letters. I was floored. When Frankie teases me he says, "You're not psychic, aunt Dar, you're psycho." Not very flattering, but I asked for a sign and I got a sign!

Not only was my daydream validated by showing me the name "Daisy," but it had come to me in a song, apropos since this was also the name of the band. Kudos to Daisy for using my daydream in such a clever way; she is a guide, after all. I guess it comes with the territory. But wait, it didn't end there. Either she thinks I'm really stubborn or really disbelieving. Some people think because I am a psychic medium I believe everything. Quite the contrary, I want validations like everyone else. I like to be sure.

A few days later I had gone to see my very dear friend, Vikki, who I have known since our infamous high school days. She had been through a very dangerous surgery, and was recuperating. It really shook me up to hear she had come close to death. Her uncle and cousins would also be visiting, and I was looking forward to seeing them again. One of them would be bringing along their first grandchild who was now a toddler.

It was great fun to see everyone, and after lunch we gathered in the living room. The baby wanted to get down. She was in the crawling stage and just able to pull herself up. She immediately crawled over to me, and I scooped her up, delighted that she came to me. After a couple of minutes, she wanted to get back down. I turned her around, and saw, printed across the seat of her pants, the word "DAISY."

On the ride over, I had been daydreaming about Daisy, this new spirit guide, and my hopes that she would help me with my readings and my quest to be a better messenger. I felt very grateful to her for weaving a connection through my daydreams, and helping me to understand how this all comes together. The more attention and focus I give this, the more it expands, and the more I write about this daydream phenomenon, the more open to it I become.

It seems there are lots of souls on the other side who are attracted to my energy during this process. Do I ever just want to put the dead on hold? You bet! When I am too busy doing readings and writing all day, there isn't much time left for daydreaming. Then my nights are vivid and filled with souls, either wanting to help me, or wanting to be helped by me. They've even gone so far as to disguise themselves as my children to get my attention.

The first time this happened, it was a soul appearing as my daughter. When I got close to her, I could see it was an old woman with a scar on her face, and when I began backing away, she said," No wait, let me explain." It was upsetting and I woke up. The second encounter came two nights later. I thought my son was standing in the living room. I could feel something was wrong and I got up and walked through the dark until I was standing in front of him. He turned towards me and I saw it was not him, but someone else. This spirit began pleading with me to help him; that "they" were trying to get him to do something. I started praying to surround him with white light, making the sign of the cross, but I was so frightened, I woke up gasping for breath.

At first I felt betrayed. I thought, "Wait a minute here, are you trying to trick me into helping you?" After a few prayers, I fell back asleep and became aware of a blue, blinking light. Its glow filled the room and I began to feel calm, almost serene. This was a presence I was familiar with. One that had come to me before in the dream with Daisy where I was being tested, and in another dream appearing as a tall, androgynous blue being, with a cap of feathery down hair, talking to me about Lydia. I like to think of them as Angels, but more importantly, I believe they exist on a higher vibrational level. When they come to me, now as just a blue light, it is always to offer insights. They assured me that these souls were not purposefully trying to frighten me, but were actually trying to make me feel safe, by using familiar faces. OK, well that didn't work!

But if I can help them, I will, and if not, I'll ask for intervention from the realm of higher vibrations—these "Blue Angels" if you will. And I never forget to say, *"Thank you."*

I do want to emphasize, though, that souls who come to visit are most often not frightening. They are mostly loving and comforting, familiar or not. It's just when you spend as much time as I do staying connected to the other side, sometimes a scary one slips in. But they just seem scary because they are so unexpected. There have been times when I was visited by what felt like dark energies, in the early days of learning how to open up to my psychic side, but they don't come asking for help. They come to challenge and provoke. And it took me quite a while to learn to stand firm when faced with huge, scary, shadow figures. Did I emphasize the scary part enough?

But I learned to believe in the power of divine protection, to stand unyielding and surround myself with God's love and light, and call on Archangel Michael and his army of angels. And I believe in the power of prayer. I pray that the souls who come to me come with God's permission, and that I am kept under God's protection.

So now I know when visitors appear in my daydreams, or show up at night while I am sleeping, it is most likely to ask for help, or offer encouragement. Look at that word, enCOURAGEment. Courage is at the root of it, and sometimes that's what it takes to stretch our views, move past our self-imposed limitations, and open ourselves up to receive the guidance, inspiration and acknowledgement coming our way from these glorious Angels and souls.

Chapter 5

CLOUD DANCING

Reality is wrong. Dreams are for real.

~ Tupac Shakur

Are daydreams real? Absolutely! Are night dreams real? Well, when you wake up with a smile on your face, feeling like you've just had a conversation with your grandmother who passed away years ago, and the scent of her face cream is still lingering in the air, for me that's as real as it gets.

I absolutely believe that when we sleep and dream, we leave our bodies. And there are seemingly lots of possibilities to where we go: meeting up with other souls on the astral plane—a level of higher consciousness—the past, the future, alternate realities, different dimensions, or maybe our soul's own version of heaven.

Most of us have experienced the sensation of falling while we are asleep and dreaming. We wake up and wonder why we never hit the ground. There have been many theories postulated about this, but I believe this is our soul, coming back into our body, after a night of cloud dancing! Maybe a little more dramatic then daydreaming, but the same nonetheless.

One night I was having a lucid dream, a state where you know you are dreaming, and you are "aware" within that dream. I knew I was sleeping, yet I could look down and see myself lying there. Even though I was out of my body, I could feel what was happening to it. Suddenly a huge force pushed up against my back, like an invisible presence trying to work its way in. I was flooded with panic, and wondered if it was some scary entity trying to invade my body without my permission. I thought if I tried hard enough, I could just push it right out through the front. I could see and feel my hands clasped together, and I tried to lean into my arms, readying myself. At that very moment, I felt a rush in my face and arms and it seemed as if I'd been hit with a tremendous gust of wind. I bolted awake. Instantly, and with great relief, I realized that it was my soul, not someone else's, coming back into my body. I caught a glimpse of my soul returning, before my physical body was aware of it.

My mother and I, to this day, have shared an amazing array of dreams and astral travel. While I was growing up, my mother always talked about her dreams and encouraged us to do the same. It wasn't unusual for her to tell us about deceased relatives, especially the aunts she was closest to, who had come to visit her during the night. I have a vivid teenage memory of the morning she woke up in a panic because she had dreamt of babies, her signal portending death. She started pacing the floors, visibly shaken. We all tried to go about our morning routine but you could cut the tension with a knife. Then the phone rang and her dreaded premonition came true: she was told her very dear cousin had passed away. I remember it like it was yesterday.

Another recollection I have is the day our neighbor died. Mom woke up that morning and told us about a dream she'd had. In it, she left the house to go to work, and had a funny, prickling sensation in the back of her neck. At the end of the alleyway that separated our house from our neighbors, was a gray-haired woman standing with her arms open wide. She looked at mom and said, "Joe died last night."

It was pretty upsetting for her, but she finished getting ready for work and left the house. As she was walking down the alley, she started feeling the same sensation in the back of her neck again, but this time it was for real. There, at the end of the alley was Mrs. Ihms, our elderly, gray-haired neighbor. She was standing with her arms open. She wrapped them around mom and said, "Joe died last night". Joe was her husband of many years.

Mom's premonition came as no surprise to us. We had been neighbors ever since she and my dad first bought our house, before I was even born. Living in Jersey City, with many houses separated by just a small alleyway, it was hard not to be in each others lives. This was Joe's way of saying goodbye.

One recent morning, I called my mother intending to tell her that I'd been dreaming about her cousin Mary who lives in Virginia. In my dream, mom and I were trying to comfort her. She was very upset that her daughter, who was a member of the National Guard, was being deployed overseas. This, by the way, was true. I naturally assumed that after I told mom about Mary, she would either tell me she had just spoken to her, or received an e-mail from her. But before I was able to say anything, mom jumped in and said, "I had the strangest dream about Mary last night." She told me the details, and then I told her mine. We were both pretty stunned to find out that we'd had exactly the same dream, right down to being in the same empty house. It was pretty eerie.

I guess mom and I both felt the need to reach out to Mary, and if distance kept us from getting to her while we were awake, we'd get there while we were sleeping. [As I am writing this, an e-mail pops up on my computer screen from my mother. She is forwarding me an Easter greeting, and when I look to see who it originally came from, it is Mary. We haven't spoken about her in months. So if you think our Angels and spirit guides aren't always watching and waiting in the wings, think again!]

Just as our soul travels while we dream, it travels while we daydream. Our soul leaves our body and the outside world becomes invisible. How can that happen? How can we leave and return in a matter of seconds and not be absolutely stunned by the experience?

It is because daydreaming comes to us as naturally as breathing. We aren't meant to be continuously aware of the mechanics of it happening. We just need to focus our awareness of what is important about it when it does happen. The experience itself is usually very subtle, like the vibrations of ripples on water after dropping in a pebble, or the sound from a harp that hangs in the air after a note's been played. We completely lose any sense of time or place. Our soul leaves and comes back, and I marvel at the ease with which we are able to regain our focus and pick up where we left off, as if nothing has happened. Then there are also those times when it is not so subtle.

I was driving home on a bright Saturday afternoon, but the weather did not reflect my mood. I was fed up, frustrated and feeling totally and completely sorry for myself. I was lonely, tired of giving and doing for everybody else, and wondering what had happened to my spirit guides and my Angels. I thought, "Who cares about my needs and wants, does anybody up there even remember my name?"

I came out of my daydream and slammed on the brakes, inches away from hitting the car in front of me that had stopped at a red light. I focused on the license plate. In large letters was the name "DARIA", my name. I closed my eyes, gave myself a moment and looked again, just to make sure it was real. Yes, there it was, "DARIA." Talk about getting a direct answer to a question! A scene from the movie, "Moonstruck", where Cher smacks Nicholas Cage and shouts, "Snap out of it!" ran through my head.

I sheepishly said, "Thank you" to those on the other side for putting me in the right place at the right time to get that message, and to my soul, for bringing me back from my daydream not a moment too soon. This was a good lesson for me because even when doubt rears its ugly head, it's important to know that our Angels, spirit guides and loved ones on the other side are using every means energetically available so they may help us.

Although most people have knowledge of Angels, and many believe their lives have been touched in some way by Angels, many of you aren't familiar with spirit guides. These guides are souls who may or may not have had a life here on Earth; not all of them have. Their mission is to help us from a higher vibrational field, to literally guide us as we navigate through life. Our guides may change over the course of a lifetime, but be assured; help is always there for the asking.

When I am giving a reading, I sometimes get messages from my client's spirit guides. Most times I can get a clear picture of who they are, what they are called and whether they lived on Earth. They sometimes like to appear as they were during a favorite lifetime. When an odd name comes up, I am sometimes riddled with a nagging sense of doubt, and wonder if people will think I make this stuff up. But I give it as I receive it, no editing allowed, and when one particular guide told me her name was Willa, I thought, OK, here we go again. Imagine my amazement the next morning, when I picked up a magazine, one I usually never read, and the first page I opened had the name WILLA in big, bold letters written across the top! It was like hearing my guides saying, "What were you thinking! You can't do this work if you are going to doubt yourself."

So if you doubt whether daydreams are real, I say they are as real as the nose on your face. If you have ever seen images from NASA—I love to go on their web site—you'll find a dazzling array of pictures and articles filled with vivid details and information of the constantly-evolving nature of our solar system and beyond. Can you imagine there once was a time when we thought ours was the only galaxy? Now their numbers seem infinite. The images of the planets, or the surface of Mars, or stars forming, seem miraculous, so close you feel like you can almost touch them. Guess what, we have!

Every day the mystery of the correlation between thought and matter unravels a little bit more. One day, passing between dimensions may be commonplace, and the idea of using daydreams to facilitate that mundane. This leaves me in awe and makes me wonder about the immeasurable possibilities that lay before us as human beings, the secrets contained within our species, our DNA, our universe and beyond. It all lies in our perception and our ability to unravel these secrets.

A tiny dot in the night sky turns into a massive giant when seen through the lens of the Hubble telescope. A swirling dance of lights and colorful gases becomes a star. A black hole, objects with such strong gravitational pull that nothing, not even light, can escape their grasp, are to me one of the most intriguing of all. Robert Naeye, of NASA's Goddard Space Flight Center, describes black holes this way: "The black hole is accompanied by a companion star in its journey through space. The two stars orbit around each other. The companion star is blowing off large amounts of gas in a gusty wind, and some of this gas is trapped by the black hole's powerful gravity. This material is destined to fall into the black hole and disappear from the universe."

For me, this is a great analogy to illustrate the complementary relationship between reality and daydreams. As we traverse life, they orbit around each other. Reality is like a bright star whose light can be seen and felt; and next to it is the black hole, where daydreams manifest in what seems like a void. On one side we are awake and alert, and when we slip through to the other side, we are trance-like and dreaming. But it doesn't make daydreams any less real; it's all in our perception. What we need to do is to embrace them both, give them equal measure in what we let influence us, and how we weigh our decisions.

I believe we live in a purposeful universe where we exist as co-creators with God and are continually evolving. Quantum physicists have proven that consciousness creates reality. By changing our perception and embracing the idea of this duality, we can open ourselves to immense soul growth, and accomplish our Earthly mission. We are, after all, eternal souls who have chosen to come to this Earth plane, bringing with it challenges and life lessons. Unfortunately, we don't bring along a magical plan to solve every problem, otherwise what would be the point of the lessons? What we do have are daydreams, and the guidance, inspiration and acknowledgement they bring with them.

Chapter 6

PERCHANCE TO DREAM

He does not need opium; he has the gift of reverie.

- Anais Nin

If you look at the definitions of the words daydream, dream or dreamt: "a state of mind without proper perception of reality," "effortlessly fall into a reverie," or "something to indulge in" [doesn't that sound delicious!], it is interesting to see that they are interchangeable. It takes no effort to daydream, it just happens; whereas, we usually go through some kind of preparation before we sleep. We take care of our pets, bathe, change into pajamas, shut off the lights, turn on the dishwasher, read, watch television to lull us off, or whatever other rituals we engage in; unless, of course, we are completely exhausted and fall asleep against our will.

Most people don't go to sleep specifically to dream; they sleep because they are tired, and it's the body's way of rejuvenating itself. Dreaming is the mystical experience that accompanies it.

Daydreaming, on the other hand, happens anywhere, anytime, and with no effort on our part. It is our soul's way of rejuvenating itself. The big question here is: do messages go back and forth between our dreams and our daydreams?

I was asleep, and dreaming that my house was filled with people. There was such a crowd. They weren't just milling about; they were standing in line and waiting to speak with me. I noticed two in particular. Near the head of the line was a tall, slim woman, nicely dressed, with her hair done and an apron on. She reminded me of the housewives that appeared in popular television shows when I was growing up. They seemed to do all their housework in high heels and pearls, and never looked rumpled. The other was a teenage boy who was turned around, holding a bottle of beer, talking to a taller young man standing behind him.

I became really agitated and wondered what they were doing in my house. Then it came to me: they were all waiting for me to deliver messages for them. I reminded them that they were not supposed to be here. They did not have permission to come to my house and take over like that. I woke up utterly exhausted with the thought that something was about to happen.

While I was going about my morning routine, I found myself daydreaming about a friend and client named Maryann. About an hour later, as so often happens when you start to become aware of your daydreams, she called. Maryann belongs to an organization that was interested in having me speak to their group about my experiences as a psychic medium and to give random readings. I agreed.

I began to suspect that the souls who had come to me in my dream "belonged" to these people, and I had been daydreaming about Maryann because she was the conduit between us.

On the night of the event, I began talking about how and why I came to be a medium. I didn't get very far, before the souls on the other side jumped in. I made a joke to the audience about their not playing fair, and began to do readings. Right from the start my suspicions were confirmed.

I immediately saw the teenage boy from my dream, the one with the bottle of beer, who had been standing in line. I walked over to a woman whom I felt he had come to connect with. I asked her if she had known a boy, around sixteen, who had the name Paul, but I felt this was his second or last name. I knew he had been drinking when he died, because he was showing me the beer. I felt that it had been on or near railroad tracks, and saw a water tower in the background. I also heard the name of a girl that had been there who might have been his friend.

She replied that she did know this boy, back when she was in high school. He was sixteen, and his second name was Paul. He had been drinking, and he died on the railroad tracks, near a water tower. She also recognized the girl's name—it was his girlfriend.

The woman couldn't understand why he would come to her, as they were not that close when he was alive. I explained to her that he had been waiting for any opportunity to come through, and this was it. When I told her how he felt about his passing, and the things he wanted to say, she understood how important it was for him. I also told her not to be surprised if she came across someone related to him. There are no coincidences and our guides will help the people we are supposed to meet cross our path.

The next soul to come through was the nicely dressed woman from my dream, who was there for her daughter-in-law. She wanted to comfort her by letting her know that this woman's husband, her son, was with her. I guess she figured he wouldn't speak up for himself.

Obviously, this was an elaborate plan coordinated from the other side for all of our souls to interact, and my daydreams and my night dreams were part of that plan. But although this may seem extraordinary, it really isn't. It happens in little ways, many times throughout the day.

So if you don't remember your night dreams, does that mean you will daydream more? Lydia says, "Our night dreams are a manifestation of our daydreams." I like to think of daydreams as being the abridged, blink of an eye version of what our guides are giving us, like a movie trailer, and our night dreams are the extended, full-length version. That idea resonates with me.

My father tells me he never remembers his dreams, but I think forgetting dreams is a habit that can be reversed. An easy way to do that is have someone or something wake you up when you are in a deep sleep. Then give yourself a moment and your dreams will come rushing back.

My friend, Fran, says she doesn't remember her dreams during the night, but when she wakes up in the morning, if she falls back asleep, her dreams are so vivid they scare her, they seem "too real." Either way, they both still daydream, everyone does.

I suppose many things can affect our ability to dream; things like changes in schedule, constant interruptions, emotional upsets and illness. Many people don't want to have dreams that remind them of people or events from the past, unresolved issues, or loved ones they've lost. My brother, Greg, a psychologist, has discussed this with me, and he says, "I think when people suppress their dreams, they are suppressing their emotions. They might not be comfortable with the feelings that accompany the dreams, so they tune them out."

Some people don't like the fantasy aspect of dreaming. They want to feel they have control over every aspect of their life, and they loose this control while they are dreaming.

So if you are shutting out your night dreams, are you also shutting out your daydreams, thinking them impractical or a waste of time? Or do you over-compensate by analyzing them away, without any thought for how they make you feel. Remembering them both can bring you insight and guidance.

There has been much written about dream analysis, but I can only tell you what my feelings and beliefs are. I believe that when we dream, our soul leaves our body behind to rest. We are still anchored to it; we don't keep floating away like an astronaut whose life line is cut and he disappears into the abyss of space. It's more like a reprieve for our body and refreshment for our soul. Without the constraints of a body, our soul can resonate with a higher frequency.

I can tell you I have had some fabulous lucid dreams. Dreams in which I could fly, feeling myself soaring over places I knew, and some I didn't. I've been on other worlds and seen people and animals that were entirely out of my realm of reality. I call these my "dreamscapes." I've been other people: men, women and children to whom I have no connection, and I've met family members, some who have passed on and some still alive. I find it interesting that if I'm dreaming of someone who is older, they appear as a younger, perfect version of themselves.

You might have had similar experiences connecting with other souls while you are dreaming. Well the same thing can happen while you are daydreaming. You become aware you are daydreaming, as you are daydreaming, and then it's important to try to recall and remember the details. Here is an example: my friend Vikki asked me to go to New Orleans with her. She has a son living there who is attending law school and was going down to see him. She booked a beautiful hotel room, had a car at her disposal and knew we could have some fun while he was in his classes. All I had to do was get myself there. Now New Orleans is a place I've always wanted to visit, especially with Vikki, as we always have so much fun together. But for some reason or another I was always missing the proverbial boat. I gave it a moment's thought, but with thousands of dollars worth of dental work looming in the near future, I didn't think it very likely. Vikki jumped in and said, "Don't say no; just think about it."

Well I no longer focus on what is *not* possible in my life. I focus on what *is*. I like to keep myself open to every opportunity the universe throws my way, so I agreed to see how things would unfold. Every day I focused on how much I would love to see New Orleans, but with no expectations. Then one morning, I was standing at the kitchen sink and found myself daydreaming about the French Quarter. All of a sudden, "Delta Airlines" popped into my head. I stopped what I was doing to fully engage my thoughts and I remembered that I had sky miles I'd never used and completely forgotten about. I went online and found I had just enough to cover the trip. An added bonus was this: since the flights are limited when using sky miles, I would have a very long layover in Cincinnati. It just so happens that I have a medium friend who lives there. Even though we have known each other for years now, talk and e-mail all the time, we've never met face to face, just through pictures. I called her and it turns out she lives five minutes from the airport and this was our chance to meet. So not only do I get to take a long-awaited trip, I get to visit with a close friend, all thanks to that simple message in my daydream.

During the night when I dream, I find myself—or my soul, however you choose to look at it—spending a lot of time in "school". This is always a place I am not familiar with. Sometimes it's in a setting that is extremely futuristic and sometimes it's more traditional, where everyone knows me but I don't know them, and I am there to be instructed or tested. Nothing surprises me anymore. I remember a very vivid dream where I was "graduating" and I was with legendary football player, Joe Namath and actor, Jim Carey. I thought how strange that I would be with these two men. But even during my dream, which was very lucid, where I felt very awake, I had a feeling that there was something we shared in our souls, something elemental we had in common and now we were advancing to the next level at the same time.

The next day I was watching television, and who comes on but Joe Namath. I can't remember the show or why he was on it, I just remember that he had a certain sense of spirituality that resonated with me. Now just for the record, my only connection to the esteemed Mr. Namath was when I was seventeen and I went on a date to a football game. We sat in the freezing cold because my dad had tickets and my boyfriend wanted to watch him play. What we girls will do to impress a boy. But that was the extent of it.

When I mentioned the dream to my sister, Stephanie, she told me she had just read a story about Jim Carey and how in his younger days he had written a check to himself for millions of dollars and put it away in his wallet, until some day he could cash it. Ironically I had been reading about the laws of attraction and manifesting good things in life and was thinking about doing something similar. It's just the number of zeroes on the check that may have been different!

I remember how surprised I was by their company in my dream, but I thought, why not, who knows what's possible. Through my work I have come to understand that we are all souls here on Earth to accomplish a mission, and so I look at celebrities as just people having challenges like everyone else. Maybe we were on the same level of spiritual development and our souls were learning in unison. I just know that we had successfully completed what we needed to learn there and, maybe one day we will meet again to find out why, either here or in our dreams.

So if you wake up with someone on your mind, give yourself time during the day to sit and let your mind wander. See your thoughts blow away like leaves in the wind and let your soul take over. You'll find they *will* come back to you again in your daydreams, and believe me when I say each time it happens, it gets easier. You will benefit from each and every one of the sojourns when your soul takes flight, whether it be daydreams or night dreams, whether you remember them or not. You do not have to be psychic, or a medium, and if you try your best to be open and receptive, you can garner much help and information. Remember that just because you may not remember your dreams or your daydreams, doesn't mean that your soul is not enriched by where it went, who it met, or what it learned.

You might think that our guides can become exasperated by the way they have to work so hard because we always on the go, until we practically fall down. But rather our Angels and the souls on the other side are patiently waiting for us to daydream, to get out of our own way so they can pay us a visit, and they will use our daydreams or night dreams interchangeably to get their message across. By taking these steps you can help make their job a little bit easier:

- Let go of the fear that you may not like what you see or feel, because if it is coming to you, there is a reason for it.
- Trust that it all has a deeper meaning for you on a soul level, so if you feel afraid, ask God and the Angels to surround you with white light, protection and love—a kind of spiritual armor.
- Keep a notebook or a recording device with you during the day or next to your bed at night. Even most cell phones can record a short

message. When you have a daydream, or wake up during the night, you can record it or write it down.

- Create a daydream journal to help you make sense of it all.
- When you catch yourself daydreaming, focus and retrieve it. The more you do this, the easier it will be and the clearer it will become.
- At night, get yourself to bed on time, and shut off the television and music so you can sleep without distractions.
- If you use an alarm to get up, set it a little earlier so you can take a few minutes to allow your dreams to filter through to your mind.
- Don't jump out of bed in the morning as soon as you open your eyes and immediately start thinking about all the things you have lined up to do during the day.
- Close your eyes, relax for a few minutes, you will find your dreams coming back to you, in small snippets, or large chunks. If you fall back asleep, repeat those steps again when you wake up. It may take time, but eventually you will remember.

Believe me when I say that if you wake up during the night and you recall a vivid dream, or during the day you are stopped in your tracks by a stunning daydream, if you don't stop and write it down, there is a very big chance that you won't remember it. I can't tell you how many times I've come out of a daydream, focused on trying to remember what it was about, only to forget. Our lives are so busy. Why not make things easier for yourself if you can. One thing I will say is that if you do forget something from a daydream, don't be discouraged. If you are meant to get the message, it will return…especially at night.

Chapter 7

SOMETHING LOST, SOMETHING FOUND

Those who lose dreaming are lost.
- Australian Aboriginal

Anyone who has ever lost anything knows the power of daydreaming. I laugh when I think of how many times I've stashed something away in a "safe place" and each time completely forgotten where I put it. It was so safe even I couldn't find it.

When we lose something, we go into search mode, trying hard to remember the last time we had it or how we could have misplaced it. We stress, make promises to the powers that be, and scour every nook and cranny, with no results. Out of exasperation, we finally surrender to the thought that either it's gone forever, or to the hope that one day it will miraculously show up.

And then it happens: that magical moment when we let go of thought, slide into a daydream, and there it is, appearing in our mind like a snapshot. It's the moment the light bulb goes off, the moment that I like to call the "AHA!"

My mother didn't believe in wasting time on retrieving lost articles. We had what she liked to refer to as the "junk drawer." Anything that didn't have a place of its own went into the junk drawer. It was large, and usually so full it would take some time and real rooting around to find what you were looking for. Most times you did. But if by some chance it wasn't there, my mother would always say, "Don't worry, forget about it. It will come to you". And it always did, whispered in a daydream.

So why not use this tool on a conscious level. When I lose or misplace something now, I skip over fretting about it. I walk away, try not to think about it, and wait until I can daydream it into existence again. Seems easy? It is.

A few years back, I had been going through a very stressful time, and during it, I managed to misplace some money. After an extensive search, I gave up any hopes of finding it and eventually forgot all about it. My friend and psychic mentor, Lydia Clar, was coming to New Jersey, and although I spoke to her frequently, I felt a reading with her was in order to get me back on track. Besides, it would be great to see her again, and with her hectic schedule, that might be the only way it would be possible.

It was a very expensive time for me. I had gone through a divorce, closed my business and bought my current home. I didn't have much expendable cash, and wouldn't take advantage of our friendship by telling her so. She's very generous and would have told me to come anyway. So there I sat, feeling very blue and completely out of sync with my psychic self.

Eventually, I went back to what I was doing, and started daydreaming about the change of seasons and my wardrobe. I thought, "I'll pull out my spring clothes, and put the winter ones away." I don't have much closet space so I'm always shuffling clothes around.

I went into my bedroom, opened a drawer and began pulling pants out, when I noticed something stuffed into one of the pockets. Lo and behold, there was the money I had lost, safely tucked away. It was the *exact* amount; yes, let me repeat that; the exact amount I needed for my reading. You'll never convince me this universe isn't a mystical place and daydreams aren't a way for helping that magic happen.

Let me also say that there are some things we lose that are meant to be lost, things that we are not meant to hold on to. They might carry some kind of negative energy or vibration that our soul can feel, but we may not be aware of it on a conscious level.

When everything was made by hand, the energy of the maker passed into the objects they were creating. We were more attuned to vibrations, and by holding something we could feel if love and care went into it. Now almost everything is made by machine. The energetic connection is no longer there and I think along the way we've become desensitized by this. When an object comes into our possession, it may take some time before we know how it will affect us.

I once did a reading for a woman who was very upset, because a ring her mother had given her was accidentally thrown away. She had given up any hope of getting it back. She loved her mom and missed her very much. She blamed herself and was carrying around a lot of guilt. But as she was telling me this, I saw a disturbing family scene. Her mom was showing me that she had been quite meek in life and didn't take a stand against an angry husband when she needed to. Her ring carried that vibration and she knew that her daughter, who was much stronger, shouldn't be wearing it. It had been lost for that reason. Her mom, with the help of her guides, arranged the circumstances for her to lose the ring, and now wanted to release her of any guilt she was feeling about it.

It is important to remember that we are all energetic beings. If you have ever been standing next to someone who has died, you know that their energy is no longer there. You can no longer feel it. Their body is right in front of you, but it seems like an empty shell. Their essence, their soul, their energy is gone.

We have an energetic exchange with everything we touch, and therefore our possessions, especially ones we handle or wear all the time, like this ring, become imprinted with our energy and vibration. When we give our possessions to others, that energy can be passed along with it. That is why many people say they can "feel" their deceased relation around when they wear something that belonged to them. Sometimes this is not always a good thing.

I myself have experienced this vibrational "essence" many times. After my grandmother, Esther, passed, I was given her wedding ring. It had a beautiful filigree design, was lacy and delicate. As a child, I used to twirl it around on her finger, to look at the flowers etched in gold. As an adult, studying jewelry design, I admired the craftsmanship. I loved my grandmother very much and was delighted to have her ring.

I slipped the ring onto my finger; it was a perfect fit. But soon after, I found myself frequently daydreaming about my grandmother, and the pictures that came to me were always sad and heavy, leaving me feeling depressed.

I knew that as a young girl, Esther came to America to join her father, leaving her mother, sisters, and brothers behind in Italy. Stories of her father, my great-grandfather, always fascinated me. I was fortunate to have known him. I was a very young child during our Sunday visits, but I remember him as a kind and quiet man who didn't speak much English. Instead, we communicated with our eyes.

In his youth he owned a mercantile business, a large store in Panama, and he traveled the world buying merchandise. When he decided to go to America, he went alone and left his wife and children to follow later. Esther was the first one he sent for. As a successful merchant, his family had the benefit of a privileged life at home in Italy. The story goes that when Esther came here to join him, she lived with her aunt, her father's sister, who was jealous of the comfortable lifestyle the family enjoyed. Her aunt sent her to work in a commercial laundry, where she severely injured her arm, which then had to be amputated. I remember how much she hated that word. She was all of eighteen years old. She married my grandfather, who adored her, and although I know she loved him very much, there were many times in her marriage where I know she felt helpless and frustrated, especially as she got older.

I finally made the connection between my moodiness and the piece of jewelry. I was picking up my grandmother's feelings of melancholy, imprinted in the ring. I know there was a lot more to her than sorrow and I wanted to remember happy times. So I decided to take it off and sadly, I put it away. My depression lifted. If I hadn't taken her ring off, she might have arranged from the "other side" for it to go missing. I am hoping, if I ask for her help, that she might help clear it, and after some time has passed, I'll try again.

On the other hand, I was given a cameo that was past down from my great grandmother to my grandmother to my mother to me, since I was the oldest girl in the family. This felt wonderful. It's a beautiful broach that was worn on special occasions, celebrations, and important events. The energy imprinted on this cameo is warm and loving. I passed it on to my oldest daughter on her wedding day.

So if you don't know the history of a piece, regardless of whether it's a small personal item, or something as large as a piece of furniture, you should try to open up your senses to it and "feel" it for awhile to understand its vibration. When you are around it, let yourself daydream and don't disregard any strange pictures that might come into your mind. Then remember the old axiom: "When in doubt, leave it out."

If you lose something, trust that your soul knows best. Maybe it was meant for someone else to find, someone who will benefit from it more than you. I love these lines, written by Walt Whitman; "Nothing is ever lost or can be lost. The body sluggish, aged, cold. The embers left from earlier fires shall duly flame again." It may be gone for now, but your daydreams might bring it back. I know if I find myself daydreaming about my grandmother's ring, I'll take that as a sign to give it another try.

There is also a flip side to forgetting; it is remembering. There is so much more to daydreaming than meets the eye, and I never expected that there would be a wonderful side effect that happened when I became consciously aware of my daydreams. It is *forgetting to remember*. Does that make sense? Let me explain.

I became aware that the more I tuned into my daydreams and the more I started relying on them instinctively and intuitively, the more I started remembering things at exactly the right moment. One day I noticed that these reminders were popping in as daydreams, just when I needed to remember them the most. By *letting go* of worry, I began to accept that daydreams were becoming like little alarm clocks, setting up alerts and signaling me at precisely the moment I needed them to. Worrying went right out the window. Gone were the little notes I'd scribbled everywhere to remind myself of what I needed to do. Instead, I experienced a leap of faith.

I've never been extremely time-conscious, never wore a watch, or used an alarm clock. I've always relied on my intuition to get me up and out and bring me to where I'm supposed to be when I'm supposed to be there. But something about this process was different. This surpassed intuition and took it to another level. So I decided to put daydreaming to the test.

I addressed the powers that be—my guides and guardian Angels—and asked for their help. I was going to be completely trusting for an entire day that the tasks I had set up for myself would come with their own reminders. I sent out a positive affirmation they would float into my mind at precisely the right moment. You know what; they did, it worked! I kept at it, one day leading to the next, asking, trusting, and paying attention. After a few days, I knew that if I kept my mind free from worry, as much as possible considering the challenges life throws our way, I could replace that worry with trust, and just let my daydreams do their work.

You can do this too. With practice, anyone can. I even gave myself a test one evening while I was watching television.

There was going to be a TV show on with a musical tribute to Diana Ross. I grew up on the Motown sound. My two sisters and I would put on a record by The Supremes and we would lip sync, do a little routine, all the while arguing over who should be Diana Ross.

I was looking forward to seeing her part of the show and listening to the songs with delightful anticipation. She was just one of a few honorees, but hers was the only part I wanted to see. I decided then and there to give this daydream intervention a real test, so I set my intention, and then began watching a different show on another channel. I became quite absorbed in the story, and completely forgot about the tribute. Suddenly, poof, there it was; a picture of Diana Ross in my head. I picked up the remote, changed the channel, and there she stood, being applauded just as her musical tribute was about to begin. I couldn't have timed it any better if I had set my watch—which I don't wear, by the way.

Since then, I have only had one instance where I felt let down. Not by the power of daydreams as tools for reminders, but in myself for getting so stressed and distracted that I was blocking them.

I had an appointment one evening to do a house clearing. I had gotten a call from a client who believed there was "something" or "someone" in her home. She was very distraught and asked me to try to validate her feelings by connecting with this presence, and hopefully, to help them move on. I had a crazy, busy day, to say nothing of the nervous anticipation I was feeling about walking into a house that was very likely haunted. All day long I would find myself daydreaming about a young girl who was upset, and crying for help. It left me with the pervasive feeling that she knew I was coming, and she was connected to this house. So in my distraction, I forgot a bottle of holy water that I had wanted to bring along.

Now I should interject here that I grew up with a mom who insisted I bless every car I bought, every train or plane I set foot in, and every apartment or house I lived in. Old habits are hard to break, so one of my mottos is: "When in doubt, bring out the holy water and ask for a blessing."

It wasn't until I was on the way there, driving in the car with my team and plenty of time to spare, that I let out a sigh and finally relaxed. And that's exactly when the daydream came to me. I saw the image of the bottle and knew I had forgotten it. My state of anxiety had blocked me from receiving it.

You see, it was the act of relaxing that brought through the daydream. Being able to relax is essential to being open for daydreams. Worrying is very constrictive, and is compounded by more worry. In other words, if you are in a state of anxiety, the act of worrying itself sends a message to your subconscious that you cannot trust yourself. You'll never let your guard down and you won't be able to relax or daydream.

This lesson further reinforced my belief that if you try to maintain a calm equilibrium, even in the midst of stressful times, your capacity to daydream will help retrain your mind and body to de-stress. If, through relaxation and meditation, you can give yourself over to daydreaming, you open a conduit between your mind, body and soul that allows you to trust in yourself and to trust in your daydreams. Eventually, you'll lose the lists, and those serendipitous moments that allows you to see and feel how truly special daydreams are, will become more frequent until they are the norm.

The simplicity of this astonishes me. *Relax, trust, daydream and remember.*

Chapter 8

FORGET ME NOT

Those who loved you and were helped by you will remember you when forget-me-nots have withered. Carve your name on hearts, not on marble.

~ Charles.Spurgeon

Ian is my son-in-law, married to my daughter, Chelsea. He had a great aunt, Eleanor, who passed on a few years ago. Nonie, as her family affectionately knew her, was an incredible woman, widowed at an early age, and one of the first women to work on Wall Street. She had tales of adventure, pictures from exotic lands, and Ian adored her.

The other night, I was driving with my friend, Fran. We had spent the day together and were pretty much talked out. I sat daydreaming, as I wasn't driving, and happened to look up, just as we were passing a billboard. On it was a picture of a woman holding a pack of cigarettes. It looked like a really old advertisement, so old, that I wondered if it was real, or if I were seeing it psychically. It brought to mind the image of Nonie.

I mentioned this to Fran, telling her the story I had heard from Ian, about how Nonie had worked as a cigarette girl in a nightclub when she was young. We talked about the old movies of the 1930s where glamorous women in little hats and satin outfits walked round the tables asking, "Cigars, Cigarettes?"

The next morning, I was unpacking some dishes I had picked up in an antique store. I often collect old china to cut up and use as mosaics. The color and design seemed strangely familiar. They reminded me of a small creamer I had. I turned a dish over, to look for a mark or pattern name, and stamped on the bottom were the words, "Forget Me Not."

I found myself daydreaming about a time right after Nonie's passing, when I met with Ian and his family at her house, to try to psychically connect with her. After an evening of receiving messages, making connections, getting validations, and some tears and laughter, Ian gave me a gift. While he was packing up her belongings, he came across a small pitcher. He knows I am an avid collector, and I have a group of small, antique creamers, so he gave me the pitcher as a memento.

I went to find it, wondering why I would be daydreaming about it now, and if it had a pattern name or mark on it. I found the pitcher, turned it over, and there on the bottom, were the words "Forget Me Not." I called Ian to tell him what happened, and we had an emotional moment, reminiscing about Nonie.

That evening, I got a call from Chelsea. When she arrived home from work, Ian related the story about the pitcher, and she wanted to tell me what else had transpired.

When Ian brought the mail in that afternoon, he stopped to browse through a catalog. An unusual bracelet caught his eye: flowers set in resin, connected with links. It was unique, something he hadn't seen before. It was called a "Forget Me Not" bracelet. But that wasn't all. At the end of the day, he sat down to watch some TV. He was scrolling down the cable television guide, looking for the time of a particular show. When he found it, he clicked on the episode information, and the title of the show appeared. It was called "Forget Me Not."

I was astonished to think that all of these messages were coming in the same day. I knew Nonie was using my daydreams to give Ian some very special validations. I asked myself why.

At the time, Ian was starting up his company, Maxx Technologies, and was under a great deal of pressure. Nonie was a very accomplished woman, and Ian held her in high regard. Knowing she went to such great lengths to reassure him, to let him know he wasn't alone, that she would be around to offer guidance and support from the other side, helped him immeasurably.

So now the words, "Forget Me Not", have been established as Nonie's calling card, and Ian pays special attention when he daydreams about her.

Soon after that, I was walking around the town of Madison, where my son was attending school. When he wanted to come home for the weekend I'd drive up to get him, since he couldn't have his car on campus. It's a lovely town, so instead of heading right home, we'd meander about downtown, or have a meal.

On this particular afternoon we ventured into a little shop. While I was wandering around, daydreaming about Ian's upcoming birthday, I found myself drawn to a beautifully shaped vase, high on a shelf. As I got closer, I could see there was an inscription on it that read, "Forget Me Not" encircled with flowers. With Ian's birthday approaching, I knew this was Nonie's way of joining in on the celebration. It was yet another validation that Nonie is still with him, still coming through in daydreams. So I bought two. One I kept for myself, as a reminder of the power of daydreams, and one I gave to Ian as a birthday gift. On the card I wrote, "Happy Birthday, love from Aunt Nonie."

What I have come to find from experiences like these is that daydreams may not always be literal, but are often filled with symbols. When an Angel, spirit guide, or loved one is working with our energy and trying to use our daydreams to send us a message, they sometimes establish a symbol that they will use over and over. It becomes their "short hand"; their way of saying, "Hi, I'm here, now you know it's me, so let's get down to business."

Since ancient times, symbols are, and have always been important representations for humanity. We find them everywhere: early cave paintings at Lascaux, Egyptian hieroglyphics in the pyramids, religious and tribal iconography, cultural representations, national flags, right down to a symbol as simple and graphic as a road sign that transcends a language barrier.

Symbols can enhance the senses. For the sight impaired, Braille becomes a symbol to feel through your fingertips; and for the hearing impaired, signing becomes a symbol for voice.

We each have our own symbols with personal significance, meaningful only for us. Part of what I do as a medium is deciphering the symbols given to me from souls on the other side and passing that information along, either as a validation that a loved one is trying to connect with you, or as a way of getting you to recognize your symbols. These symbols become their language.

A friend of mine who lives in Ireland found a site where "I love you" was written in just about every language known to man, even sign language. It got me thinking about symbols as the special language I have developed with the "other side" to help me exchange their messages of love. These symbols include images, memories, songs and sounds, smells, feelings and emotions, words and phrases, and they appear as a daydream.

But the language I have developed with my guides, spiritual family and all the souls who come to pay me a visit, either in service to you, or for myself, are not exclusive to psychics. It's meant for everyone willing enough to be open to this process of receiving what are essentially messages of love and guidance, expressed through symbols. All through life they emerge as signposts, sometimes small, sometimes really in your face, giving you a little "heads up" about what you are doing or about to do. Daydreams become the vehicle that provides you with the symbols you need to choose the right path.

Lily of the Valley is a deliciously fragrant little flower that is highly symbolic for me. Not only because it blooms in May, right around my birthday, but it also reminds me of a time when I climbed the fence around the Lutheran home to pick some of these tiny treasures to make a nosegay for my junior prom.

The first home I bought had them blooming all over the yard. Each spring I would fill my house with vases of them, and then wake up sneezing my head off and have to give them all away to my family. Life is ironic, isn't it?

When I sold that house and found my present home, I wasn't surprised when I spotted the Lily of the Valley growing everywhere. What has always been odd is that it will grow profusely in my yard, but never in the neighbors yards, not even a straggler. That's what makes this symbol uniquely my own. It was my Angels' way of saying, "Here is your place to call home, a place to find peace and contentment, a place you can fill with love."

One day, when I move from this house, as I will eventually do, I'll be looking for symbols to be my compass. They are my "yellow brick road", there may have lots of twists and turns, but they will always lead me home.

Not every symbol will be as obvious as Nonie's "Forget Me Not," or my Lily of the Valley. But with patience and perseverance, if you ask for help and learn to decipher them, *your* daydreams will bring *your* symbols, and with them will come *your* guidance, *your* inspiration, and *your* acknowledgement.

It has been many weeks since I wrote this, but I wanted to add these amazing experiences that occurred over the past few days concerning Nonie.

My friends Nancy and Fran were here for dinner the other night. Afterward, we sat in front of the computer to look at a web site for antiques that Fran had found. While she was busy searching for it, Nancy noticed the "Forget Me Not" vase that I mentioned earlier. I told them about Nonie and how that phrase has become her calling card. Just as I finished, not more then an instant later, Fran found the site. I pointed to an icon that looked interesting, so she clicked on it and brought up a picture of a locket in the shape of a heart. It was big enough to plainly read the words, "Forget Me

Not" engraved on the front of it. Needless to say we were stunned. I knew immediately that Nonie was trying to communicate with me.

I called Ian who told me his grandmother Charlotte, Nonie's sister and constant companion, had been admitted to the hospital and the prognosis wasn't good. I tried to reassure Ian that whatever happened, Nonie was around. I thought the mystery was solved.

On Saturday, two days later, Fran was going to be in an antique show and I offered to help her. She suggested I get some things together and bring them along to sell. While I was daydreaming about what to bring, I remembered a drawer where I had stashed a few small collectibles, some old post cards from the early 1900's among them. As I was taking them out, one fell from my hands onto the floor. Written across the card in beautiful, embossed letters were the words, "Forget Me Not." Wow, twice in one week! I hadn't looked in that drawer in over a year, and had no recollection of what the post cards looked like. In fact, if I knew it were there, I probably would have given it to Ian as a memento long ago.

Once again, I tried to reach him, but couldn't, and found out from my mom that he was headed to Delaware to see his grandmother, so I beseeched Nonie to watch over them all.

Saturday came, the antique show was quite busy, and when it was finally over I was able to listen to the voice messages on my cell phone. One was from my daughter saying that Charlotte had passed away that afternoon. It was sad news. She was a lovely, gentle woman who had lived to be 93 years old.

On the way home from the show I kept daydreaming about the post card, wondering if there was a message on the back. When I arrived, the first thing I did was to find the post card, turn it over and see if there was an inscription. There was. Hand written in delicate, old fashioned script, it said, "I am coming on Saturday."

Nonie and Charlotte were as close as sisters could be. Both of them were widowed at a young age, and spent most of their lives living together until Nonie passed away a few years ago. I'm sure she knew when Charlotte was getting ready to leave this Earth, and the post card was her message to us that she would be there, on Saturday, ready to welcome her sister home. This story is a wonderful testament to how the bonds of love we share in life, through the power of daydreams, are never really broken in death.

Chapter 9

A MATCH MADE IN HEAVEN

Charm is a way of getting the answer yes without having asked any clear question.

~ Albert Camus

Yesterday morning, I found myself daydreaming about a friend I'd met a few years back. It had been quite some time since I had last seen her, many months in fact, but you know how some friendships can be, it doesn't matter if time has gone by, you just pick up where you left off. So I was not surprised when I heard a knock, and found her standing at my front door.

We fell right back into the rhythm of friends, talking about our children, who they were dating, and who was breaking whose heart.

Somehow our conversation was steered toward boyfriends from our youth. The ones we knew for a short time, maybe dated only once, but for some reason, their memory always stayed with us. Almost everyone has a story to tell about missed opportunity, the wrong choice or the one that got away.

I started telling her about a time when I lived near Rutgers University, where I was enrolled to take classes. I think I was probably nineteen at the time. I shared an apartment with a friend, who had also moved there from

Jersey City. A couple of guys lived in the apartment across the hall, and every time I'd walk past, I would hear someone playing a guitar.

It didn't take long for us to meet, and soon we were spending a lot of time together. One of them was named Gae. He was always playing music on his guitar, and he was the one I gravitated to. Gae was very charming and charismatic; a nice looking guy who just had a way about him. His energy was magnetic. No matter where we went, when he walked into a room, all eyes were upon him.

We spent most of our time together in a group of friends. He was very popular with the girls, and everywhere we'd go, they would come up to him, either flirting or admonishing him for not calling them. He was always bragging to his friends about his latest conquest, but that didn't stop me from thinking that if we were able to really get to know each other, alone, away from his entourage, it would be different between us. There was something that drew us together, and we both knew it. I thought this force would overpower his ego, but I was wrong. Sometimes, in my youth, my emotions had a way of overriding my psychic antennae. We went on one date together, and it became apparent that his reputation meant more to him than having a relationship with me, so I ended it before it even began.

Our friendship went downhill from there. I suspected he and his friends were using drugs, but I guess they soon felt comfortable enough to start using them in front of us. I also noticed cars began following them around, the kind of cars with undercover policemen in them. I decided I'd had enough. I wanted to leave the apartment building. I was picking up negative vibes everywhere I went, in the whole area in fact, and I wanted to go home. So I withdrew from school, packed up my apartment, and left.

As I was telling her the story, she started getting this funny look on her face. She told me she had an uncle who was named Gae. I told her the Gae I knew was really named Gaetano. She replied that was also her uncle's name. I asked her how old he was, and she said he probably would have been around my age, but he died. She commented on the fact that this is a very unusual name, and how odd it was that we both knew someone with it. She asked me what town I was in when I knew him, and it turned out to be the same town he grew up in. OK, now things were really getting weird. I said I remembered this friend he had, a big dark-haired guy he was always with, who was really sweet. She replied, "Jay," and I shouted, "Yes!"

She told me that the person I described; musical, charming and charismatic, fit her uncle to a tee. Everyone who knew him was affected by him. Unfortunately, the darker side of his character won out, and he passed away at a fairly young age. The last time she saw Jay was at her uncle Gae's funeral.

She was as astonished as I was. We had worked together for a year and had an instant connection from the moment we met, but who knew that we were also connected by Gae. Could he have been instrumental in getting us together in the first place? I'm sure he was. We talked about the fact that he had never come through in any of the readings I had given her. How she had been daydreaming about me that day, and on the spur of the moment, decided to come to my house. If she had chosen to ignore that daydream, all of this would never have transpired; a lost opportunity.

I believe she was led here because daydreams are doorways for guidance, inspiration, and acknowledgement from our loved ones. I'm sure Gae saw this as his opportunity to be recognized as the soul who brought us together. Maybe the date was significant, or someone in their family was sorely missing him and it was his attempt to get them a message. Or maybe he wanted us to finally understand that right from the beginning our meeting was no coincidence. It was a connection made through the guiding force of love, a unifying force that never dissipates, never goes away, even in death. That love is an eternal bond that reaches from soul to soul, in a never-ending cosmic dance. And because she was receptive to the message in her daydream, she was able to have this experience.

When an event as powerful as this happens, the impact reverberates through your life, and, in turn, touches the lives of those around you. I'm sure she shared this story with family, and for each person who hears it, there is the prospect of being profoundly affected by it. It presents you with an opportunity to open your mind, push your boundaries and explore your daydreams as credible tools. It helps you to understand the dynamics of spiritual interconnectedness, how Angels, spirit guides and family who have passed can be our teachers, and how you can share that message with others. It creates a great spiral, encircling each person it touches, that can lead you to a life rich with spiritual fulfillment.

We have a vast array of spiritual help just waiting for us if we ask for it. From the beginning of time as we know it, Angels have been messengers delivering that help. Lately I have been hearing my Angels loud and clear. As I was waking up one morning, I heard a very distinct voice say "This is the universal truth." Ok, I thought, you've got my attention. So I asked, "What is the universal truth?" The voice answered back, "We are all one."

You may think this is a strange way to start the day, but each morning, before I get out of bed, I ask Archangel Gabriel, "What do I need to know today?" He jumped the gun a little bit this morning, but I could feel the power behind the words.

That truth is simplicity itself. We are energy, and you cannot separate energy. There is interconnectedness between our inner and outer selves, and each other; the simplicity of which becomes astounding. As Archangel Gabriel made very clear to me, the universal truth is that we are all one, and love is the unifying force. I remember a quote from author, J. Holloway, who said, "Too often in our society; we neglect the importance of creating meaningful connections with the world around us. I believe that, as soulful beings, we are made to share ourselves with each other."

I've also come to understand the subtle differences in the energy of the messages coming from Angels, spirit guides, and souls on the other side.

The information that comes from the Archangels has a profound, inspirational feeling about it. You step out of your body for a moment. You are given, to put it very simply, a statement, like a truth expressed, a gem of knowledge, a "knowing" meant to inspire a thought or create a way of thinking. Almost like a muse it gives you something to reflect upon. They send ripples through your vibratory field ever so gently and suddenly there it is. The saying, "Filled with grace" comes to mind. The Angels seem to come at the times I feel most open and relaxed; especially upon awakening or after a meditation when I am naturally in a daydream state.

The messages coming from spirit guides seem to have a more intuitive feeling about them. They come as answers to questions, bringing messages to help clear away stumbling blocks, or immediate, in-your-face signs to keep you moving in the right direction, and conversely, to tell when you are not. They sometimes "break into" your daydreams in a more forceful way, especially when you aren't paying attention, or are presented with a life-altering challenge. They may show you psychic premonitions or give you a feeling in your gut to rethink certain decisions, or help you to understand the outcome of taking a certain path. And when you aren't staying open to your daydreams, they will even put obstacles in your path to get you to change course. Daydreams help them to do what they do best: guide.

Messages coming from the souls of our loved ones who have crossed over have a mystical or sentimental feeling about them. They resonate with a certain vibrancy and excitement, yet there is a familiarity about them. They will use our daydreams to affect our senses, causing us to feel a gentle touch, smell a fragrance lingering in the air, or see an image, flashing like a picture across a screen. They will come during extremely emotional times, bringing feelings of joy or comfort, and to erase doubt. They move easily between daydreams and night dreams, validating their presence. Their messages almost always carry with them feelings of love and acknowledgement as if to say, "We are here, with you now, and always."

Look into your daydreams and, in time, mysteries will unravel and truths will be revealed. Honor the spiritual bonds you have with those souls trying their best to present you with moments frozen in time, rich with information, presented to you in a daydream; the kind of information that you never in your wildest dreams, could have made up. Messages that could lead you to the kind of inconceivable connection like the one my friend and I shared through Gae. For however brief a time we knew and loved him, he reached

Daria Justyn

out to us through our daydreams, because he knew the truth that on a soul level we are all one.

    Thank you, Gae.

Chapter 10

FIREWORKS OR FIREFLIES

What is life? It is a flash of a firefly in the night. It is the breath of a buffalo in the wintertime. It is the little shadow which runs across the grass and loses itself in the sunset.

~ Crowfoot

I believe in the veracity of the souls on the other side. Souls, who have agreed to help us in life by inspiring and instructing us. They help us to identify our own unique signs and not veer too far off the path we are supposed to be traveling. It can't be easy for them. We have so many distractions in the course of just one day, let alone an entire lifetime, it's a wonder they can help us at all. That is why daydreams are so important. Our Angels have only a moment when the outside world disappears; just enough time to send us a thought or an image. When we develop our ability to access the inner world of our daydreams, we become effective creators of our own lives. When we can capture and focus on those moments, we can avail ourselves of their help.

My son, Evan, who is very philosophical, shared this thought with me: "If thoughts are energy, and we are surrounded with this energy, then our soul can choose which thoughts we need to create and channel that information to help us. We just have to learn to read the signs." The way to do that is through our daydreams.

I grew up going to Catholic schools. We were always reading Bible stories about someone getting an incredible sign like a burning bush, food multiplying, or water turning to wine. The stories were always so vivid for me, so real, I felt like I could see it all happening right before my eyes. Whenever I felt something strike a chord in me as not quite right, and questioned the "official" interpretation I got from my teachers, their answer was always the same: "It's a mystery!" So I would go back into my daydream world and arrive at my own conclusions. But I remember thinking, "Why don't miracles happen for us? Why would they only happen thousands of years ago and not now? Are we so beyond redemption that God doesn't see fit to waste miracles on us? Or are there a finite number of miracles to go around, and they were used up by the people memorialized on those pages so long ago."

The dictionary describes a miracle as: "An event that appears to be contrary to the laws of nature and is regarded as an act of God; or an event or action that is amazing, extraordinary, or unexpected."

Back then I thought of miracles in terms of loaves and fishes, and the parting of the Red Sea. Now I understand that they can appear in small gestures and not just on great gales of wind. They are alive and well and living in this century. We've just been looking for the fireworks, when we should be looking for fireflies.

Think about it; fireworks make incredible displays of light, fleeting but beautiful. If you know where to look in the sky, and for how long, you will be rewarded with a night sky filled with blazing bursts of light, color and fanciful imagery.

Yet if you were ever standing outside at dusk, surrounded by lightening bugs, you wouldn't even notice them until their tiny lights began flashing around you. Peering through twilight, you're not sure where the lights will blink next. But if you stay open and responsive, you'll find your gaze magically going to just the right place, at the right moment, to catch a dazzling array from natures little lanterns giving you their evening light show.

And so it is with daydreams. You can't just look for the fireworks; you need to be open for the obscure, for the little fireflies. You might see something subtle, or you might see something extraordinary.

There are so many astonishing events happening to us all the time that we shrug off as coincidence. We call them luck, destiny, or a twist of fate, but when you examine these "chance happenings" on a deeper level, you'll find they can be diminutive miracles, disguised as happenstance. Fireworks are obvious, fireflies are subtle. The way to understand these subtleties is to explore your daydreams, look at the symbols and intercept the messages.

What I've done here is present you with some examples of what happened to me, so you, too, can learn how to recognize the miracles that are happening in your life as well; not just the fireworks, but also the fireflies.

While I was in the process of divorcing, I put our house up for sale. Trying to find another home for my family seemed like a monumental task, but I was up for the challenge. I felt I had the right realtor helping me. I can't really remember what brought me into Lila's office, but I connected with her instantly. She was very open, knew I was a medium, and understood when I said a house had bad vibes and I didn't want to go in.

She came to my home one day with papers that needed to be signed, and noticed my dog and my cat. She told me she also had two pets—a dog named Shadow and a cat named Angel. Alrighty then! It's an understatement to say her jaw dropped when I told her that my dog was Angel, and my cat was Shadow. I believed without a doubt she had been sent to help me; definitely fireworks!

When I finally did find the right house, I knew it. I didn't get the house immediately, but I wasn't disappointed. After an exhaustive year of searching, I had come to believe it would happen when the time was right. Then two weeks later, after I dealt with some family affairs that needed to be completed,

Lila called to tell me the house was available again, and was mine for the asking.

After I bought the house, two things happened to assure me I was meant to be there. Just a few days after moving in, I went outside to take a break from the endless unpacking and sit on the stoop. Anyone who grew up in Jersey City knows what it means to sit on the top step and watch the world go by.

I soon found myself daydreaming about my friend, Audrey's, mother. I didn't know Helen all that well in life, but had heard from her on more then one occasion after she passed, especially while I was house hunting. The first house she led me to was on Union Street. I had been seeing her name all day long, and Union was the name of the street she lived on with Audrey and her family. Well that house turned out to be not quite right, but I still felt her presence. I'm sure it was just meant to delay me until this house became available.

When I realized I had been daydreaming about her, I said out loud, "Helen, if you had anything to do with helping me find this house, I send you my gratitude and my love."

A little while later, some of the neighbors came to introduce themselves. The first was an elderly widow who lived across the street. Her name was Helen. Her house was newly built, and she was happy to be living two doors away from her friend, also named Helen, whom she had known since kindergarten. While we were speaking, her friend Helen's husband ambled over. He was having difficulty and used a walker, but being the polite gentleman he was, he introduced himself and welcomed me to the neighborhood. I guess seeing the commotion, the woman who lived in between them decided to come over. When she introduced herself as Helen, the fireworks began exploding in my head. Three neighbors named Helen; I was incredulous.

Later on in the day, Angel, Shadow and I went for a walk to explore the river beach. I still couldn't believe all the "Helens." I didn't get farther than the corner, when I came upon a woman working in her front yard.

She walked over to me and in a gesture of friendship, extended her hand. Although everyone I had met was lovely, it was nice to finally meet someone my own age. When she said "Hi, I'm Helen," my stunned reply was, "Did I move into the twilight zone?" She laughed and guessed I had met the other three Helens. She said I wasn't crazy, but people probably wouldn't believe me when I told them. We laughed, exchanged some pleasantries, and then I continued on my walk down to the river's edge. I felt fulfilled, amazed and grateful to Helen, for coming to me in a daydream, and for acknowledging my gratitude. I knew that my family and I were safe, and where we were meant to be. Thanks Helen for those fireworks.

The other occasion happened in an upstairs closet. It was large enough for me to get in and move around, so I went in to clean the shelves before I started putting things away. I don't know why, but I started daydreaming about the flower shop my mom opened while I was growing up. I was the oldest girl, and being artistic [lucky me], I worked there on and off, from the time I was sixteen—taking time off for school and travel—until I was about twenty seven, when mom closed the business. My memories were really good ones. My brother and I talked my parents into buying a VW van for delivering flowers, but our not so secret agenda was to take it camping on the weekends, and we even tried taking it to Woodstock. On the holidays, we all worked long hours and we'd argue with my father to lock the door against the endless parade of last-minute customers. During the week our friends would come and hang out since my dad worked in New York and my Mom didn't mind. That business became quite a creative outlet for me and gave my family the opportunity to have lots of adventures. I really liked our customers and I especially loved reading the sentimental notes they wrote on the little message cards that we sent along with the flowers.

My focus returned, and I felt so blessed because there wasn't one inch of this house that frightened me, not even the dark closet. I happened to glance down and noticed what looked like a small paper stuck between the wall and baseboard. I reached down and pulled out a tiny envelope with the name of a florist across the top. A card was tucked inside. I recognized this immediately as one of these message cards. I could still see the holes where it would have been pinned to a bow on a flower arrangement. It was addressed to the family who sold me the house, and signed by the original owner. When I pulled the card out of the envelope, it said, "Welcome to your new home!" Chills ran through my body, going off like the lights on a swarm of fireflies.

I found that card, a perfect sign, at the perfect moment, and even though it wasn't a burning bush, it was enough of a miracle for me. The fact that I'd been daydreaming about the flower shop was a wonderful validation for me that I had found a place to live where I felt truly blessed.

As you can see, every sign is not glaringly apparent. Some are very understated, which means you need to live your life being aware. Daydreams don't always come with bells and whistles, but they do come with meaning and intention. You need to find yours. Daydreams are a way of highlighting those important moments in your day and throughout your life. Every time you make an important decision, it's done in the present moment. But in retrospect, weren't there some mystical events that led you up to that moment? Someone or something you couldn't explain away, that appeared at just the right time? And maybe each time you tried to convince yourself that it happened by chance?

I guarantee you it was no such thing. You were being guided by those inspirational thoughts that were brought to you via your daydreams to help you stay focused and stay on track. But with the images in daydreams coming and going so quickly, like little fireflies, it's easy for them to be there and gone before you've even had time to process them. So I have trained myself to pay attention to my daydreams and follow the energy to find the highlight in the message and the intention behind it. You can learn to do this too.

Everyone who calls me, asking for my help as a medium has a reason for doing so. There may be one big reason, or an accumulation of little ones. They may think it's all their idea, but their Angels and guides have been planting those seeds in their daydreams and helping to orchestrate the events that led up to our meeting, sometimes with our help, and sometimes with our resistance.

As I've said before, doing a reading is like having a series of daydreams, and invariably, during the reading, something comes up that I feel is the highlight of our time together, the part that you really need to pay attention to. It is always accompanied by a surge of energy that I recognize as their signal, letting me know that this is the real reason we've been brought together.

When I am reading for someone and I am in my messenger mode, I let everything go once I've said it. In fact, most times I can't recall what I've said five minutes after saying it. But every now and then, something comes back to me, a kind of recognition if you will, and it always happens when I'm daydreaming.

The other evening I was sitting in my living room, and began daydreaming about a woman who came through from the other side for her daughter. When she received the particular message that was the highlight of her reading, the reason she was guided to me, my indoor wind chimes rang. You see, I keep solar wind chimes inside my house. When left in a window, they absorb energy from the sun on a small solar cell, and then they'll chime randomly, but on a rather frequent basis. If you place them under a lamp, they'll chime on a very regular basis, so much so that I was ready to throw them out the window. So I placed them in a spot that was neither by a window nor under a lamp. What I found is that they'd sit there all day and night, hardly ever going off, but whenever I was giving a reading, they would chime. I soon realized that the souls on the other side were manipulating them to get my attention. It worked. In the beginning I was skeptical because I know that the solar cell absorbs some light from the room, but by recognizing what they were doing and being open to it, I expanded my means of communication. Now I've gotten used to the chimes ringing in the midst of a reading, highlighting something I've said or a message I've just passed on for them.

On this particular evening, hours after our reading had ended and I found myself daydreaming of her, I thanked this soul, for giving me a message that I hope resulted in tremendous joy for her daughter. At that exact moment, my chimes started ringing. Don't ever think they aren't grateful for our recognition.

After that, I began to notice the way the chimes would ring, not only during readings, but while I was daydreaming. I began paying attention to the timing, and to my utter amazement, I was able to identify what daydreams my guides wanted me to be especially conscious of. It was their way of saying, "Highlight this daydream and find the intention behind it."

Does that mean that you have to run out and buy wind chimes? No. It means they will use whatever means available to them to get you to pay attention to the messages coming in your daydreams. If that means lights blinking, phones ringing, door bells buzzing, pictures flying off the wall or tiny miracles; so be it. The question you need to be asking yourself is: "Am I aware, am I paying attention?" Because once you become aware, there is no turning back.

Chapter 11

IMAGINARY FRIENDS

*When babies look beyond you and giggle,
maybe they're seeing angels.*

~ Eileen Elias Freeman

It's natural for children to daydream when they are young; as natural as breathing. They'll live for hours in an imaginary world, a serene reverie, still more connected to the other side than to here, without the constrictions that come with being a "grown up."

While children are still young, their souls are free to roam, and they have little difficulty in seeing their Angels and guides, and feeling the souls of spirits around them. When their daydreams turn into conversations, we say they have invisible friends, and call them "imaginary." These companion souls use the doorway of daydreams to get through, even with the smallest of messengers.

Children have a natural psychic ability but as they grow, with pressure to adjust to the "norm," they gradually tune it out. Memories of life on the other side fall away like leaves in the wind. They forget that extraordinary existence, visions of Angels and spirit guides may fade, and gradually they become enamored with other things. Some of this "forgetting" is the soul's way of keeping you singularly focused on your life and where you are going, not where you came from. This makes it possible for you to get on with things in this lifetime, or else, you wouldn't want to stay.

This isn't always the case though; some children revel in their connections with the higher realms, and never out grow it. Their ability to daydream grows with them, and they embrace a life communicating with the other side. More and more of these children are souls who have come to usher in the great changes that will accompany the rise in spirituality we are all witnessing. Either with the help and encouragement of their families, or in spite if them, they nourish their psychic side, and welcome their Angels with open arms.

My sister called recently and asked me to "tune in" to a little girl who was the daughter of a friend. Her parents were worried because she seemed distracted by something in the room that they couldn't see. They felt their little girl had a gift, apparent even at such a young age. Her mother was curious but concerned that her daughter wasn't getting enough sleep. She began to worry when objects that were out of the little girl's reach landed on the floor. She expressed her concerns to my sister, who then asked for my help.

When I focused my thoughts on the little girl, I saw a man dressed in old-fashioned clothing. I could see that his hair was parted and combed, and I saw the starched collar of his shirt under a jacket. The name, "Jacob Henry" came to mind, and the year 1865. I saw a little girl, who I felt was his daughter. She had been killed in an accident, possibly a fall. I saw a broken latch on a window frame, gas lamps throughout the house, and the green walls of a nursery. I also saw a woman in a black outfit, the kind women of the day wore when they were in mourning. She seemed to be Jacob's sister. I gave this information to my sister and she said she would pass it along to the family.

The next day, my sister called me. She was with her friend who wanted to validate some of what I had seen. When the woman got on the phone, she told me that her daughter's nursery was painted green. Her mother's house, where she grew up, and which was close by, also had a nursery for her daughter that was green. It was an old house with gas lamps and broken window latches before they modernized it. She remembered seeing something carved into one of the basement walls, so after persuading her reluctant mother to accompany her, they ventured into the basement together. There, carved into the wall, were the initials JH [Jacob Henry?], along with the year 1800 something, she couldn't make out the last two numbers. She asked me why this spirit was around her daughter, and if she was in any danger.

I felt it was a case of mistaken identity. I could tell that somehow, Jacob felt responsible for the death of his daughter, and transferred these feelings to this little girl. Whether he believed this girl was his daughter, or he was just safeguarding her so as not to suffer the same fate was unclear. But I knew that his soul was there, benevolent, harmless and very apparent to this little girl. I also believed that if they petitioned the other side for help, especially from Jacob's sister and his real daughter—the name Annie came to mind—that they might be able to convince him to make the transition and move on. I told her what she and her husband needed to do to help this come about.

During our phone conversation, something else happened: I began connecting with a different energy, and started getting messages from a man who had crossed over. From his name, how, when, and where he passed, and the nickname he went by, there was no mistaking that this was man was her uncle. Although Jacob was there, her uncle claimed he was the one responsible for knocking things down, trying desperately to get their attention. He made it clear that he was the one who had arranged from the other side, for them to speak with me.

It seemed from the way he passed and the time of year, the Christmas holidays; it was still very painful for his family. He was very close to his niece and wanted to let her know his spirit was light and relieved of the burdens he carried with him while he was alive. He had messages of love for his daughter and other members of his family.

This woman was dumbfounded, but she said if anyone would try to come through, even if it meant making a ruckus and scaring them out of their wits, it was her uncle. She thanked me, and said she would relay the messages to the rest of her family.

It felt very gratifying to be a messenger for this soul, to bring his niece joy and encouragement, and to bring his family some form of closure.

A few evenings later, my sister called again. She wanted to tell me that her friend had shared the messages from her uncle with their family, and since then, objects in the house had stopped moving. She had also taken my advice about helping Jacob to move on, and since then, all was at peace in the house.

One evening, when it was her daughter's bedtime, she told Jacob that he didn't need to stay there anymore, that the girl would be safe with her family, and that his daughter and sister were together and waiting for him "in the light." She made a point of telling my sister that she never once said this out loud, only in her mind. When she kissed her daughter goodnight, the little girl looked past her and said, "Bye, bye Jacob."

Even before all of this transpired, this woman believed that her daughter had a gift; and as her mother was going to do whatever she could to foster and nurture this ability. She understood how her daughter was instrumental in not only helping a soul to move on, but also in getting her uncle's message delivered. This message brought peace to a family in desperate need of validation. She embraced her role as mother and protector by turning fear into action.

Children have an open doorway while daydreaming. It is through compassion and appreciation that they will learn to keep that doorway open to communicate with their Angels, spirit guides, and souls who need their help, and not be left hiding under the covers. Daydreaming can be their refuge and a place to learn that each and every one of them has infinite potential. Daydreaming can bring light and understanding, and empower them when their daydreams are validated.

It is very obvious to me that this present generation of children is different. I believe they are greatly-evolved souls, meant to be on earth at a time when we are facing global challenges. Some may never have been here before, and clearly are having difficulties coping. Some are so highly advanced we don't know how to deal with them. These new souls are being labeled as having every disorder under the sun, when it is we who must realize that our evolutionary process calls for change; and we who must change with it. It is time to embrace a different way of thinking, learning, and teaching. I am asking you to open yourself up to the possibility that we have an innate tool in daydreams, whose potential we have been unaware of, until now. Potential that is limited only by our ability to open our minds, our hearts, and our imagination. There is help being offered from a place of higher consciousness that was here when we were children, and even more so now. For the sake of all of Earth's children, embrace the change and keep the doorway open.

In the words of J.W. Whitehead: "Children are the living messages we send to a time we will not see."

Chapter 12

PURR--FECT SOULS

Who can believe there is no soul behind those luminous eyes!

~ Theophile Gautier

There is a cacophony of song outside today. Birds are in the trees, on the wing, large flocks celebrating the melting ice and the sun glistening on the river.

I have no doubt animals daydream. You just have to look at them in that dreamy state of repose to see it. Even animals living in the wild, or living in cities on their own, struggling to stay alive, manage to play, rest and daydream. I am convinced there is a rich tapestry of musing and contemplation going on when their needs are met, and so much more so for our pets who can loll around all day, basking lazily in the sun. I wonder; what do they daydream of?

I find animals irresistible. Not just for their resourcefulness, unconditional love, ability to sooth, and amazing quality of inventiveness. But also for their intuitiveness, the way they can look at you and respond without you having uttered a single syllable. It is this very quality that I believe helps them to communicate with us through our daydreams.

Animals have come to me in readings. My own animals that have passed on, have shown themselves to me in various ways when I needed it the most.

When I found out that my beloved cat, Shadow, was fatally ill, I had three consecutive dreams. In each dream, one of my dogs or cats that have passed on came to me by jumping up on my bed. I could feel the bed jolt as they sat and looked at me as if to say, "Don't worry, we're here now, we'll be waiting. She'll find her way home with us."

Animals have very distinctive sounds, and pets, even more so, because you become accustomed to their unique voice. If you had to, you could probably pick yours out of a group just by listening. On the day of Shadow's death I heard my dog, Angel, bark very loudly at three different times during the day. It was so loud that it startled me, and her sound was unmistakable. Angel had died over a year ago. Each time it happened I had been daydreaming. It was a chilling experience.

Angel, Shadow, and I used to take walks to the river together. We would stroll to the waters edge and stare off, each in our own daydream. We shared a feeling of contentment, watching the river, feeling the sun, the wind and listening to the seagulls. I knew that Angel's presence made Shadow feel safe enough to venture out of her familiar territory and follow along with us.

When they were at home, Angel, a big, black, lovable mutt, and sweet, little Shadow would curl up together on a blanket. To see them napping next to each other was endearing. Whoever said dogs and cats don't get along should have seen this pair. They were priceless.

After Angel died, Shadow seemed lost and wouldn't sleep on their blanket anymore. In fact, whenever she came to the spot on the floor where Angel died, she would circle around it, never walking through it, as if Angel's energy were still there.

When Shadow became ill and passed on, I was so lonely for my sweet little friend my heart ached. But it helped me to know that Angel and my family of animals had eagerly awaited Shadow's return home to the other side. I knew they were together again.

Daydreams can be portals for magical happenings, and one day, a few months after her death, Shadow actually appeared to me.

It was a beautiful, sunny, fall day. I was in my front yard, raking leaves and feeling very melancholy, thinking of her, how she loved hugs, and how the neighbors couldn't get over the way she walked along with Angel and me. At bedtime, she liked to climb under my bed covers, pop her little head out, lay it on my arm and fall asleep.

As I was standing there, daydreaming, something caught my eye. I looked down and saw Shadow walk right past me. It was almost as if a circle had opened up and she appeared. She took a few steps and then disappeared as quickly as she had come. I felt like I could have reached down and touched her. My mind was suddenly filled with the most vivid daydream of her continuing her walk in a green pasture, flooded with sunlight.

I knew it was that moment of daydreaming that she stood waiting for, and when it fell upon me, she used it as a doorway to show herself to me. With a heart full of joy, I sent her a huge, energetic hug and let her go. I'll see her again, I'm convinced of it.

I absolutely love the thought that the animals that were entrusted to us here on Earth are happy and whole and still feeling our love on the other side. But animals don't have to have passed on to access our daydreams. They can do it just as well while they are here, and part of our lives. I believe they have this uncanny psychic ability to be able to read our thoughts, especially when we are daydreaming. When they feel we need their assistance, and they do, or when they are in trouble, need our help or just our attention, they can use our daydreams to send us a message.

After Shadow passed, I decided to remain animal-free for awhile. I wanted to travel and not have to worry about leaving pets behind. Well, I guess the universe had other plans, because I was daydreaming one day and the thought, "Jenna's going to give you a kitten" popped into my head. I called my daughter, Jenna, and got her to spill the beans: she had rescued a tiny kitten from the garbage dumpsters near her apartment. One cat turned into two, and then three. So much for best laid plans.

Some time ago, I became very preoccupied with a furry orange cat that found his way to my yard and wanted very much to be a part of my family of cats. It was obvious he was a feral cat, and would not have any human contact of any kind. Even so, he was determined to be accepted by the cats. He showed up on my deck every morning and evening, looking for food. Now bringing in another cat—hello-this would be number four—was something I was desperately trying to avoid. I live near woods, and every season another stray comes wandering out. Our local animal shelter, Jersey Shore, has an incredibly warm and devoted staff, but feral cats that aren't socialized can't be adopted out. So it was up to me to try and help him, hard to do when every time I came within twenty feet he took off like a shot. It was through months of sheer determination, and huge heating bills from keeping the door open, that I was able to earn his trust just enough to get him to come into the kitchen for his meals. I thought if I could coax him into a cat carrier, then I could at least get him to the vet to be examined and vaccinated. On the day I called to talk to my vet about giving it a try, he disappeared. Who said animals can't read our minds? I will never again question the intuitive abilities of animals.

Fuchi, [whose name appropriately means "run like the wind"] had gotten used to my whistling as a way of calling the cats in for the evening, because he would always show up, albeit at a distance. I looked for him for days, canvassed the neighbors, and called the shelter, doing everything possible to find him. My dad came to offer help, and my mom, bless her heart, did what she always does, she said a novena. I prayed to Saint Francis of Assisi, the patron of animals and to Lillith, head of the nature angels [I like to cover all my bases] to guide him home. Nine days later, he showed up at my door, starving for a meal but seemingly uninjured. He ate ravenously, and left. I sent up a prayer of thanks and went off to attend a meeting I had scheduled. There, on a huge poster board in front of the room, was a quote about imagining the impossible. It was by Saint Francis of Assisi.

I'll never know what happened during the night, but the next morning he came back, limping, and looking badly injured. It was by the grace of God, and my telling him psychically that he needed to trust me, that he walked right into an open cat carrier. One year later, all healed from a dislocated hip, neutered and vaccinated, this cat who wouldn't let anyone near him, is sleeping peacefully on my bed looking like the king of the jungle. He has become part of the family and purrs away while I brush him.

The uncanny element to this story is that anytime I need him to come inside, all I have to do is send him a psychic message, and he shows up like magic. He hasn't missed a night indoors in over two years. I'm sure that message gets to him while he's daydreaming.

So now, when I notice one of my furry friends staring off in a daydream, I think, what can you see that I cannot? I have noticed many times while I am busy, they will break into my thoughts with a daydream. I'll stop what I'm doing, thinking, "The cats are calling me" and go to the door and there they are, waiting to come in. They look at me as if to say, "Thanks for getting the message" or sometimes, "It took you long enough."

I believe daydreams are doorways to communicate with the animals in our lives. When you find them daydreaming, send them a psychic message and watch for a response. If you don't get it right away, keep at it, don't give up. You'll be surprised at how uncannily this can work. Before you know it, daydreams will become a natural means of communication. Try it, what have you got to loose?

Everything about our world is changing with lightening speed. Spirituality is on the rise and as we become more soulful, we examine our lives, how we arrived at this moment and what is important to our evolution. Maybe recognizing that daydreams are a form of telepathy is part of that, and using it to communicate with animals is a natural extension of that evolution. Every species has its own language. It may seem far-fetched, but we share this planet, and truly engaging in learning to communicate with daydreams may become a way to cross that barrier.

Anyone out there still think animals don't have souls? Just look into their eyes when they are daydreaming.

Chapter 13

SYNCHRONICITY

*People don't come to church for preachments of course,
but to daydream about God.*

~ Kurt Vonnegut

Most people I have spoken to, say they don't pay any particular attention to their daydreams. They think it's just something that happens to them and they feel no participation in the event.

Attending Catholic schools, I spent much of my time in church, and I've often thought how easy it was to be lulled into a daydream. I absolutely loved listening to the Mass being chanted in Latin. I was in a serene place where prayers became more than just words. They resonated with a vibrancy that I could feel swirling around me, and I would drift off into my own sacred space. I would sit, watching the light change as it filtered through the colors of the magnificent stained glass windows; and with each whirl of the priest's robes, see the lights of the candles flicker in homage to my prayers. I would float away on a river of musical hymns, drifting off in a daydream, until the whoosh of everyone standing in unison brought me back. I think of something Deepak Chopra said: "God has managed the feat of being invisible and worshiped at the same time."

Daydreams may seem intangible, but they are very powerful tools. In school I was always being reprimanded for daydreaming, but in church, prayer was the meditative road that took me there. I felt part of something bigger then myself, as I plugged into the collective energy of all the souls who had gathered to pray. The funny thing was, for me, participating was a distraction. I wanted to be an observer. Needless to say, this didn't go over to well with the nuns. But I wanted to bask in all the glorious energy that resonated around me as my vibrations were raised higher and higher. Flashes of insight came to me in daydreams, and I felt an almost telepathic ability to communicate with those around me. Little did I know how this particular kind of group energy would positively affect my ability to daydream, raising my energetic vibrations to a place that felt "other worldly," and ultimately experience what I perceive as, "being in a state of grace."

As a child I never understood what that meant. They were just words about an elusive place that seemed reserved for the saints and the very holy. Now I know that when you experience that surge of energy that raises your vibrations, covers you with goose bumps, and fills your soul with awe, gratitude, and an all- encompassing feeling of love, that moment of recognition is what being in a state of grace truly means. It creates a "knowing" that resonates with every molecule in your body and lifts you to a higher place where your body and soul are one. Can you imagine if we could all embrace the reflexive power of daydreams and use this energy to create a world of synchronicity that could change the planet? I could. *You are what you daydream.*

Quantum physics has shown us that everything is constantly in motion, vibrating to different frequencies. Nothing is really solid and every atom inside us is more than 99.9999% empty space. Astrophysicists say that visible matter accounts for only 4 percent of the universe; *only 4 percent*! Einstein put it very succinctly when he said, "Reality is merely an illusion, albeit a persistent one." Did you know some physicists say we are essentially recycled stardust? So when you "wish upon a star," you are part of that star, and you are creating the answer to your own wish! Our energy is always ebbing and flowing and the thought that we are separate is simply not true.

As my Angelic messengers have said: "We are all one, and we are what we daydream."

By daydreaming, by relaxing into that meditative state, even for a moment, you allow your vibrations to resonate with the higher frequency that is outside of the physical world. It's like tuning in to a perfectly-pitched musical note. Each time you daydream, you hear another note; and when you put those notes together, you create a melody. Eventually, from that melody, you create a song; one that mirrors everything your soul has come here to accomplish.

If we all learn to resonate, or tune in, with the higher frequency of our daydreams, we can blend our songs together and create a global symphony of unity. We can each fulfill our unique role in attracting and creating what is needed to make the world of our dreams, the world of our reality.

When I presented my friend, Laura, with the idea that when you daydream, you *bring something back*, some guidance, inspiration or acknowledgement, she replied, "I really like the idea of having had a moment outside this world to a place of higher knowledge and then returning to Earth; that notion never occurred to me. I've always thought of guides planting ideas in my head, not me stepping over to meet them half way."

When I posed the question: "What is your impression of a daydream, what do you think is happening?" to family and friends, this is what they had to say:

- A thought you don't initiate
- Wishful thinking
- Regrets
- A way to keep sane and escape the mundane
- An idea with no forethought
- Deceased family members who want to be noticed
- Past, present, or future thoughts

- Our atoms popping in and out of existence
- Inspiration
- Moving between lifetimes that we are living simultaneously

Some were closer to the mark than others, but no one mentioned daydreams as a way of accessing our soul, connecting with our Angels and spirit guides, and retrieving information to help us accomplish our Earthly mission in this lifetime.

So I ask you this: what if you looked at a book as a metaphor for life, with your soul as the author? Einstein believed time does not exist, and there is no difference between the past and the future. If this is accurate, that time is just an illusion, and from my psychic readings I believe this to be true, then maybe our guides and loved ones travel these higher frequencies between our past, present and future, which are existing simultaneously. They go back and forth between the pages, using our daydreams to get us a message and help us write the next chapter. Maybe that's what de`ja`vu is—we have all been here before—and our soul is just skipping between the pages.

But attempting to learn from our daydreams can be a very difficult challenge, when in our daily lives we are never without some kind of distraction. We have television, movies, radios, and computers. We have cell phones that we carry everywhere, and text messaging when we are unavailable to speak.

So how, when our minds are constantly flooded with this never-ending barrage of disturbance, can we connect with our daydreams? The answer is by being aware and *never* disregarding the messages that come as intuitive or inspired thoughts. Because when you are dealing with the "other side" where there is a will, there is a way.

My girlfriend, Audrey, now lives in Florida, but on September 11, when the planes hit the World Trade Center, she was working right across the street. Miraculously she was not injured. But I remember the emotional pain and grief she went through, along with countless others.

I woke up one September morning, a few years later, and began working on a project, unaware that it was the anniversary of that day. I kept daydreaming about Audrey. My intuition was telling me to call her, but I really needed to keep on working, and I was constantly being distracted by phone calls. So I ignored it. Big mistake!

I went on the computer, and decided to check my e-mails. I saw that one was from Audrey. She had sent out a warning about a computer virus having to do with September 11. I thought, "So that's why her name keeps coming to me." It was a lengthy e-mail, and half way through it, in the middle of the page, was a perfect square, surrounded by a beautiful border of flowers. In the center of it was the name, "Helen", completely out of context and having nothing to do with the rest of the message. I thought it was odd that Audrey would stick her mother's name right in the middle of a sentence, especially something with such an elaborate border. The funny thing was, the border design looked *exactly* like one of the fancy stitches I had created, not long ago, with my sewing machine. I was baffled.

I e-mailed her right back to say I had been thinking about her, but was unaware of the date, and by the way, why did she stick her mother's name in the middle of that e-mail? Ten minutes later she called me. She didn't know what I was talking about. She didn't put it there, and since mine was part of a group mailing, she checked with a couple of other people and it didn't appear for anyone else. No one else saw it, including Audrey.

I forwarded it to Audrey, so she would know I wasn't hallucinating, it was really there. I had been daydreaming of Audrey, who sent me a message, who, in turn, received a sign from her mom. That's synchronicity. I believe Helen saw the opportunity, and manipulated energy—which those on the other side often do—to send her daughter a message, on a day when she knew Audrey really needed it. What I remember most is how incredulous I felt.

When we pay attention and don't disregard our intuitive feelings, we stay connected and allow the synchronicity of being perfectly in tune with our daydreams to happen. If I had listened to my daydream and contacted Audrey, Helen wouldn't have had to work so hard to get her message through.

But part of her being able to do that, is my willingness to be receptive to experiences that fall outside of the realm of "normal."

Daydreaming, connecting to the other side, connecting to our Angels, spirit guides, family members and loved ones, that is something shared by all who possess a soul, regardless of faith or beliefs. We hunger for a sense of spirituality, for that connection and the feeling of awe that comes with knowing we are not disconnected souls going through the motions of being alive, but that our soul is on a quest, an eternal journey to grow in love. One of the gifts we were given is our ability to daydream, to become conscious of our purpose, our mission, and the potential it affords us to reconnect with our soul, recharge our energy, and re-evaluate our lives, all through the miracle of daydreams.

Chapter 14

CELESTIAL CIRCLES

The world is round and the place, which may seem like the end, may also be the beginning.

~ Ivy Baker Priest

The circle is a major component in nature. It is one of the mysteries of math. Where does it begin and where does it end? We look at life as being linear. We track events in our lives on time lines, looking past and looking ahead. But I've come to realize that life is circular, and not linear, and the end can actually be the beginning. We refer to "circles of friends," and people who "move in the same circles." Hang on to your clothes, because you know eventually fashion will circle around, and they will be stylish again. We've heard the phrase, "What goes around comes around," hundreds of times. The first games we learned as children were played in circles. There are crop circles, medicine wheel circles, and the circle at Stonehenge. Of course anyone who lives in New Jersey knows how to navigate its famous traffic circles. This is the story of one of the circles in my life that began and ended with a daydream.

My son, Evan, is a lacrosse player and had been interviewed by a local newspaper. My former business was in Spring Lake, where I was very familiar with this paper; but, since I was no longer there, I hadn't seen it in quite a few years. I read the story about Evan, but didn't feel like reminiscing about the town, so I put the paper away. Later that afternoon, I was doing a chore and started daydreaming about the newspaper. I felt this overwhelming urge to stop what I was doing and go back and read it. While I was turning the pages, I saw an article entitled, "Together for Teresa." I thought they were referring to St Theresa, who I am fond of, and started reading.

A young woman, just 21, who used to live in the nearby town of Manasquan, had broken her neck in a snowboarding accident. There would be a benefit to help raise money for her recovery. With a terrible chill I saw the name Teresa Schroeder and thought, no, this can't be. I frantically called the phone number listed, and asked if this was the Teresa, whose mother's name was Jennifer, and if she had a brother, Sean, and a sister, Amanda. Even though I knew the answers would all be yes, I couldn't quite believe it.

So I went to the benefit, offered my psychic services, and was overcome with emotion when Sean came walking in. I was able to give him a big hug; something I hadn't done since he was a little boy.

When I first moved to the shore, my children were all young. I was walking down the street one day, with Evan in a stroller, daydreaming, when I looked up and saw a small boy on the roof of a house, heading toward the electrical wires. I ran up to the front door, rang the bell and Jennifer answered. It seemed Sean had a penchant for climbing out his bedroom window. I said, "Boy, do you have your hands full." We laughed and became fast friends.

Jennifer and I had a lot in common, including three small children around the same ages. We were both on a spiritual quest, and had many magical moments together, far too many to ever use the word "coincidence." Our friendship gave serendipity a new meaning.

I remember one time we took our children to a Native American pipe ceremony. It was late afternoon, sunny and clear. We sat in a circle, passed the pipe, and laughed because the children were disappointed that we wouldn't actually let them smoke it.

When the ceremony was finished, we were allowed to ask questions. Something I had read about, and was intrigued by, was what the Native Americans refer to as "the thunder beings." I asked if we could hear about them. Just then, as if on cue, a thunderbolt roared overhead, shaking the ground we sat on, and it began to pour. Needless to say, I received my answer; and we were pretty speechless for the rest of the night.

Eventually, Jennifer and I moved to different towns, then different states and drifted apart, as so often happens in life. It was when my daydream led me to read about Teresa that I knew it was time to circle back into her life again.

My daughter, Jenna, decided to go to Oregon, where they now lived, to offer help and support. It was such an emotional and exhilarating reunion for her, that as soon as she came home, she and I made plans to go back together.

Upon our arrival, seeing Jennifer, Sean, Teresa and Amanda again was like coming home. I thought, "How could we have wasted so much time apart?" As a medium, I understand that the paths we choose that bring us together, or tear us apart, are necessary for our growth, but being surrounded with people we love makes the journey so much richer.

When I returned home, I called Echo Bodine, a spiritual healer, psychic and teacher. She is the author of one of my favorite books, "Echoes of the Soul". It was with her help and encouragement, years ago, that I started writing. When she told me, "Honey, those dead people are just going to keep on coming," I knew I had to embrace my gift, and stop hiding from it. I wanted to speak with her, to enlist her help with Teresa. She has a group of advanced students she calls "Healing Pen Pals," who will send absentee healing to those who ask. Thank God, with love, prayers and the support of her family and friends, Teresa is healing, spiritually and physically.

Daria Justyn

During our conversation, Echo and I were talking about books and publishing houses, and to my amazement, she brought up Shakti Gawain. When Jennifer and I met, we discovered we shared a love of books that were spiritually enlightening, and were stunned to find out we were both reading the same book, "Creative Visualization," by Shakti Gawain, at the same time. Hearing Shakti's name and re-living that experience, brought me right back to the beginning of the circle; meeting Jennifer. Now, every time I find myself daydreaming about Jennifer, she calls. Isn't it incredible that a daydream would lead me there? I think so.

Chapter 15

WHEN YOUR MIND GOES ELSEWHERE

I saw the angel in the marble and carved until I set him free.

~ Michelangelo

When you daydream, a seed is planted in your imagination. As you become aware of it, this thought begins to expand and grow, like flower petals slowly unfurling. Imagination knows no boundaries, and the more attention and energy you give it, the more it filters its way into the forefront of your consciousness. You are inspired, you begin to imagine, and then you create.

I wonder how many great ideas and works of art started out as daydreams. Most, I think. Picasso said he painted things as he thought them, not as he saw them. Whether we are staring at a blank canvas, or a math problem, it isn't until we let go and let ourselves be inspired, that the revelation comes to us in a daydream. Then we begin to conjure up images in our mind, creating with an invisible paintbrush. We become lost in the process of setting the scene, creating the backdrop, building, inventing, like a movie and we are the editors. If we can imagine a book, we can write it; or a piece of furniture, we can build it, or a concept that puts information on a tiny little chip that changes the world, as we know it.

So when people say, "What an imagination you have," what they are really saying is, "What a great daydreamer you are."

Beethoven said whole symphonies came to him while he was daydreaming. I have heard musicians say over and over, that when they are writing songs and reach an impasse, they walk away and try not to think about it. Only then are they inspired. That elusive note or lyric comes to them like a lightning bolt, when their "mind is elsewhere." I'm sure it's the same for poets, writers, any creative endeavor really, whether you're fixing a car engine, or designing a space shuttle. But have you ever stopped to think of where you go, when your mind goes "elsewhere?" It goes into a daydream, to retrieve "soul messages" from a higher realm. Do daydreams help us imagine thoughts into existence? Absolutely.

It has been almost a decade since I opened my last venture, an arts and crafts gallery, yet one part of imagining it into existence always stays with me.

I needed, among other things, to come up with a name. Since I was selling art, it couldn't be just any name; it had to be fun, whimsical, and decidedly different from the myriad number of stores already at the Jersey shore.

Searching for the right location wasn't easy either, in little towns with lots of businesses vying for good locations.

I was walking the streets of Manasquan one day, a quaint little town I loved, and was praying for a sign that would lead me to a location I could call my own. I looked to my right, and tucked in at the end of a driveway was an adorable, tiny cottage that had been a store. In really huge letters, the words "FOR RENT" covered the entire front windows. Talk about signs; there was no way I could have passed this place and not noticed it. Even the address was odd: 134 ½. It was small, but definitely had the charm factor going for it. The rent was affordable and it began to feel like a place I could envision my dream. So I signed the lease, and the real work began.

Angels Whisper to Us

As I worked toward getting the gallery up and running, I needed a respite from weeks of making decisions, so I decided to take a ride south and spend the day at Long Beach Island. I have so many great memories of fabulous summers there; fun times I shared with my family when we would descend on the beach, with kids in tow, and more equipment then you'd need on a safari. It was the first time my brother, Mark, introduced us to Moire, the woman who would become his wife. Our very dear friends, Barbara and Bill, have a summer house there, and together we would gather for fine wine, incredible meals my mom would make, and laugh till our sides split. Bill has since passed away, which make those memories even dearer.

I spent the afternoon driving around, feeling nostalgic, enjoying the scenery and visiting shops, but one thought occupied my mind: I needed to come up with a name for my store. Time was running out, and everyone from the printer to the sign painter was on hold. I had lists of words I liked, phrases, names that had already been used, titles of paintings, anything I could think of to inspire me, but nothing came. Also, I wanted the name to be more then just words; I wanted it to evoke a special feeling. Thinking about it so much had given me a headache. My mind was empty and my ideas had run dry. I started back up the Parkway for the ride home and as I did, I thought, "That's it, I give up."

With few cars on the road, and feeling mentally exhausted, I fell into a daydream. I try really hard not to daydream while I drive, but I did, and I can't tell you how long I drove that way until all of a sudden, the phrase "Moon and Sixpence" popped into my head. It caught my attention because it literally came out of nowhere. I hadn't been thinking about it, reading about it, and I hadn't heard it mentioned anywhere. I wondered what a strange thought it was, but the fact that it came to me, out of the blue and into my daydream, caused me to sit up and take notice. I felt like I was onto something. I recognized it as the title of a book by Somerset Maugham, but there was something else. Geoffrey Chaucer and "The Canterbury Tales" came to mind. "Wow, I did learn something in high school after all" I thought. Actually, one of the highlights of my high school years was studying

English literature, and "The Moon and Sixpence" struck a chord. It would be an odd name, but it was whimsical and I thought it would pique curiosity and interest.

The following morning I headed off to the library to do some research. I confirmed that "The Moon and Sixpence" was from "The Canterbury Tales," but something else caught my eye. It was the date Chaucer was born: 1340. There were the numbers of the address to my store; 134. From the chills running up and down my spine, I knew without a doubt, that this would be its name. I felt as if my soul already knew this information, and through my daydreams, I was able to access it. I thanked the powers that be and my imagination started working overtime.

Indeed, "The Moon and Sixpence" became its name, and the store opening was a delight. Over the years, so many people told me they wandered in because they were intrigued by the name, yet stayed and came back because of how special it felt just to be there. So much more came out of having that store, from bringing meaningful new people and experiences into my life, to finding the courage, with Lydia Clar's help, to overcome my fears of being a medium and come to terms with my psychic ability.

In my daydream I was given a phrase in just an instant. But from that phrase I was led down a path, following the signs along the way, and imagined a business that I brought to life.

Those years went by with lightening speed, and so much has changed since then. Change comes so fast these days that it almost seems like time is speeding up. But time is an illusion. So if we are all here on Earth as souls traveling toward the same destination, to learn and grow through love, then maybe it's not time that is speeding up, but our energy. And if our energy is accelerating, then is it happening on the other side as well?

I believe it is. One day, a beautiful, evolved soul emerged during a reading I was giving, with an energy that felt warm and illuminating, and seemingly different from anything I had experienced before. This soul revealed to me that it was part of a "collective of souls" who had taken on a mission to *inspire* us at this pivotal time in our evolution. Our actions not only impact each other but the world as we know it, and it is becoming evident that making significant changes are crucial to our survival. Still, I wondered how they would do that and why? This soul assured me it was their mission to help raise our spirituality through *awareness*, to send us a notion, show us a sign, to somehow get out attention by planting a seed in our daydreams. And by doing so, *if we listen*, one by one, our actions would collectively work together to exponentially raise the vibrations of the planet. This would shift the delicate balance to advance our development instead of destroy it.

Just as our guides work to coordinate whatever is necessary for us to be in the right place at the right time, these souls do whatever they can to inspire us with thoughts that will help elevate mankind. They will instruct us to turn our thoughts from violence and greed, and guide us to imagining a world filled with peace, unified through love. This sounds like an enormous undertaking, but, believe me, they are up for the task; and they will use our daydreams to do it.

Chapter 16

THE LANGUAGE OF DAYDREAMS

Breathe. Let go. And remind yourself that this very moment is the only one you know you have for sure.

~ Oprah Winfrey

Daydreaming allows you to disconnect with your surroundings and connect with a pool of consciousness that is outside of yourself. It's like stepping into a gently flowing stream; you feel the water running around your feet as you slowly let go of conscious thought and what is happening around you. You become one with the sensation of the flowing water and you lose yourself to the outside world. When your mind shuts down, you enter a stillness where your daydreams can connect you to this place of higher consciousness, for within this field dwell energies that exist at a higher vibration then we have here on Earth, and can bring you information relevant to your life here and now. It is through the stillness of daydreams that you are able to access these energies and allow their messages to unfold.

Clearly, daydreams have a meaning and a purpose, and how you react to daydreaming can tremendously impact your life, so in order to better understand the message, it helps to understand the messenger. I believe that these messages can come from different sources. You can learn to distinguish these different energies, which are made unique by the singular feelings they impart. They come from Angels who wish to inspire us, from spirit guides who are helping us accomplish our mission here on Earth, and from souls we may or may not have known that have passed over, yet have information they wish to validate or share with us.

When you think about the act of daydreaming, you might ask: *"How do I tap into this energy and access this guidance?"*

Here is what you can do when you have a few moments:

- STOP the chatter in your head by focusing on your breath
- BREATHE deeply and close your eyes
- RELAX and allow your mind to become still
- IN THE STILLNESS you will begin to daydream
- FOCUS on the highlight of your daydream
- FIND THE RELEVANCE to your current situation

Daydreams have a certain cadence about them, and it's that familiarity that helps you tune into them amid the chaos of everyday life. You may already know that when your mind is either relaxed or distracted, you daydream, even though your body may be otherwise engaged. But it's much easier to daydream when not only your mind is relaxed, but also your body. So doesn't it make sense that if you consciously relax your body, you'll daydream more?

We all know that daydreaming happens anytime, anywhere, anyplace without conscious effort, but did you know that you can learn to develop your daydreaming skills? Just by learning to relax you'll learn to daydream more. You've taken down the barriers of distraction and resistance, embraced the stillness and allowed for a safe, open field where you are receptive. Here is the field of your daydreams. This doesn't mean you have to walk around like a space cadet with your head always in the clouds. It just means giving yourself permission to be still, release your thoughts and let daydreams take your soul where it needs to take go. This is where meditation is helpful.

The theme of daydreams as doorways is becoming more apparent to me day by day. When you daydream, you open a channel that gives your guides the opportunity to plant the seeds of messages in your mind. This same thing happens either when you meditate, or when you linger in that "in between place" of being no longer asleep but not quite awake. If you can learn to cultivate the art of meditation, then you give your Angels and guides a rare opportunity by increasing the times you will be receptive.

Creating time for introspection is an important part of learning to use your daydreams as tools to develop your consciousness. When you meditate you relax, and when you relax, you daydream. It's as simple as that. Can you daydream without practicing meditation? Yes, everyone does, but if you don't want the distractions of life to get in the way and you really want to access the information in daydreams, then help yourself along by learning to meditate.

Breathing is an important part of meditating. Our bodies need oxygen, from the moment we take our first breath, the one that cements our body to our soul, until the last one that sends our soul home on a gentle breeze. I visualize breath flowing in and out of my body like waves on the shore, each inhale imbuing my body with vitality and peace. Each exhale releasing negativity and blocks. It has a way of calming me down and allowing me to hear my guides and Angels in a much clearer way, because in the stillness of breath lies daydreaming.

Oftentimes, in stressful situations you might find yourself holding your breath. So now, as you become aware of this, remember to breathe deeply through your nose. Let tension flow out of your body as you breathe out. Relax for a few moments and reconnect with yourself. Each time you inhale, visualize everything beautiful, loving and peaceful for yourself and your loved ones entering your body. With each exhale project loving thoughts, circulating out to everyone, like ripples on a pond. Then let go and daydream

To learn *how to distinguish the messages in daydreams*, think about the following questions:

- Did the daydream make you feel inspired, intuitive, or sentimental?

- Did it answer a question or pose a challenge?
- Were you sharing a telepathic thought with someone that was validated later on?
- Were you given a psychic premonition?
- Did you see someone who has passed on, hear, or smell something familiar about them?
- Was your daydream followed by an extraordinarily serendipitous moment, what we commonly call a coincidence?
- Was there a message that clears away doubt or gives you an affirmation that helps you to move forward?
- Did a daydream startle you into action, empower you to change your life or achieve a goal?

It's hard to pay attention to every single one your daydreams, *but you should be especially attentive* when:

- You anticipate a change or take on a new challenge.
- You find yourself daydreaming about a person or situation and then you hear about them or they suddenly appear.
- You are trying to create something new; when you have cleared your path and are open for opportunities.
- Your daydreams take on a mystical, serendipitous quality and start bringing you inspired thoughts.
- You feel something is about to happen, or you have an extrasensory connection with someone.
- You are going through troubled times, filled with uncertainty or doubt and are having trouble making decisions.
- You find yourself repeating old patterns, ignoring your intuition and feeling you can't trust yourself to make good choices.
- You are daydreaming of a loved one who has passed on, that brings back a memory or validates a feeling.

Please trust that there is a reason for why daydreams come to you, so pay attention. Your loved ones are all around you, ready for acknowledgement and a mere thought away. Your Angels will inspire you when you need to be creative, and your spirit guides will step in and help undo the roadblocks you have set up for yourself and work to keep you on the right path. Remember, there may be pitfalls or obstacles put in your path if you need to change direction. But if you let your daydreams guide you, you'll keep you moving forward because *daydreams create an awakening that will lead you to your soul's purpose.*

Breath is the beginning of this process and the introduction to meditation. In the calm, stillness of breath lies daydreaming. Meditation can lead you there.

Chapter 17

DREAMSCAPES

No one can get inner peace by pouncing on it.

- Harry Emerson Fosdick

"Meditation" seems to be a word people hear and immediately feel intimidated by. I get this over and over again whenever I suggest it. They say, "No, I can't do it, I'm too busy, it's too weird, I don't have the space for it, I can't quiet my mind" and on and on. But I assure you *this does not have to be a daunting task.*

Meditation is a journey home, to a still sanctuary deep inside of us. It can be simple and uncomplicated; as simple as breathing, or envisioning a broom to "sweep" away a thought when it begins to intrude, chanting a single sound, or focusing on a word. You can spend five minutes, twenty minutes or however much time you need to "get away from it all." Overall you will be calmer, your intentions more purposeful and you'll find yourself daydreaming more often.

There have been countless ways written about how to practice meditation, but whatever method you choose, they all lead you to the same place: your inner self, your inner being, your soul. How do you go about preparing to meditate? It's about creating a "dream space," a place to *go*, and a "dreamscape," a place to *be*.

A "dream space" is a place where you will literally *go* to meditate. It's a place where you can be comfortable, serene, alone, undisturbed and free to relax. It doesn't make any difference if it's the broom closet or the bathtub; it just needs to be a safe haven, peaceful and quiet. That means no radio, no television, no phones, no chatty family members, no barking dogs, purring cats, children who need attention, spouses, etc. I think you get my drift here; if it makes noise or can bother you, keep it away!

You can create a space as pleasing to the senses and as tranquil as you choose. It can be as simple as a favorite, comfortable chair during a time when you won't be disturbed, or it can be an elaborate sanctuary; it's up to you. If you can safely light a candle without worrying about a wagging tail or curious little fingers touching it, then by all means go ahead. I always light a candle for two reasons: I imagine the flame absorbing any negative energy around me or in the room, clearing and cleansing it. It's also a signal that says, "I am here, please get ready to join me," to the Angels and guides who will gather round and offer support by way of the messages they will send. I also keep wind chimes *inside* the room where there are no breezes. Since energy can create movement, I know when they ring it is a gesture from the higher dimensions that I need to become aware of who or what I was just daydreaming about in my meditation.

Try to choose the same time every day so your mind, your body, and your soul become in sync and recognize that this is your meditation time, the time to let go of your mind, forget your body and connect with your soul.

Now that you have your dream space, it's time to create your "dreamscape," the place you create in your mind to just *be*.

When I first began to meditate, I found it difficult to keep my mind clear by just focusing on my breathing, so I began to create a beautiful dreamscape in my mind. I decided that if I imagined every detail, it would feel so real that with practice, I could "go there" quickly, and from there I would lose my physical self. For me, my dreamscape was a beautiful beach; for you it can be your perfect place. I would create every detail to my liking and actually "feel" everything as I created it. Of course, since this was my special dreamscape, it could be anything I wanted it to be. I've always loved to sweep; it makes me think of my grandmother. Sweeping can be such a tranquil activity, and so when outside thoughts intruded, I just swept them away.

Here is how I begin: I light a candle and as I do, I ask The Divine Oneness [an Aboriginal term for God that I especially like] to absorb any negativity I may be carrying around me, my home or my family. I ask to be surrounded with a column of white light of the Holy Spirit, the light of protection, and have my soul and the souls of my loved ones filled with love, light, grace, abundance, peace, prosperity, good health, wealth, happiness and gratitude. [You can substitute these words with any of your choosing.] Then I sit in a comfy chair with my feet on the floor, imagining magnets grounding me to the Earth so my body is stable but my soul free to wander. I close my eyes and take three deep, cleansing breaths, and with each exhale I release any tension I am holding, feeling it flow down through my body and out the bottoms of my feet to be filtered through the Earth. Then I ask the Angels to gather round me. I imagine them with little feather dusters, and they begin dusting away any negativity that might have collected on my ethereal body, or aura; an electromagnetic field emanating from the body, always in flux, absorbing vibrations from the environment.

Now I begin envisioning my dreamscape: It is a radiantly clear day. The sun is low in the sky as it is nears dusk. I can feel its golden warmth sparkling on my face as I gaze upward. The breeze is warm and gentle and as I breathe deeply I can smell the salty sea air. I'm standing at the water's edge and as far as my eyes can see, the water is aqua blue, amazingly clear but only inches deep. Off in the distance a shimmering waterfall cascades, sending up a mist filled with every nuance of the rainbow. I feel the sand, smooth and warm between my toes and the sun drenched waves lap at my feet, cool and inviting. I open my arms to give thanks and turn my palms up to receive energy and guidance as I invite my council of Angels, guides and loved ones to gather round. I let myself *be* and I'm *gone*.

After a while, with practice, it became easier and easier to create my dreamscape and lose my physical self. I would find myself "gone" for longer periods of time, and each time I came back into a state of awareness, I realized I had been daydreaming.

Then I began remembering details. Some were associated with family members and friends, here or deceased. Some were confirmations of events currently happening in my life. But just as often I was in the company of strangers. I found myself in unfamiliar places, yet I felt like I was supposed to know where I was. I was interacting with people who treated me with a familiarity that made me feel like I had a purpose for being there. The more I focused on the details, the more vivid the pictures became. One day, I finally understood that the strangers coming to me in some of my daydreams were souls who needed my help. I remembered Lydia saying that through meditation, I would learn to develop this gift I had, and my role as a medium would become clear. She was right, it did.

This next step was paramount: *I started writing*, whenever possible, everything I could recall when I came out of a meditation. Then I expanded from jotting down notes about my meditations, to keeping a journal of my dreams when I woke up every morning and finally when the light bulb went off in my head, to documenting my daydreams as well.

Whenever I found myself daydreaming, I relaxed and allowed it to happen. Eventually I was able to piece together clues to where my soul had gone and why, or who I was visiting with. I began connecting those daydreams with friends and family, people I knew or those that had just come into my life, and then with Angels and guides. I understood there was a rhyme and reason to it all, that daydreams weren't random. They were full of messages, sometimes for me, and sometimes for others.

But this is where *my* daydreams took me. *Your* daydreams will have a destination all their own. For daydreams create an awareness of what we need to reflect on, and in each life, for each soul, the reflection is different. Who knows what will come from yours.

My Angelic guides assured me that *the more you endeavor to use your daydreams as a tool to develop your consciousness, the greater the potential for soul growth.*

Meditation is an obvious way, even though it's a skill that needs to be mastered, because it happens in a natural and fluid way, just like daydreaming. But it doesn't happen over night; it takes practice. It's also important to remember that it doesn't have to be a structured event. You can meditate in the bath or shower at the end of the day, or while sitting at your child's bedside, waiting for them to fall asleep. You can turn off the television a few minutes early and sit in silence, or wake up a little before you need to. Anytime I have to sit in the car waiting for someone, I close my eyes and do a mini-meditation. And anywhere that has what I call a "serenity protocol"; like the beach, a pond, lake or riverfront, or even a secluded spot in a park where people assume you have gone to be alone, is a great place to practice meditation, so don't give up.

There are more ways than meditation to help you make sense of the information from daydreams: there's understanding about your energy and how to work with it, learning to distinguish between the voice in your head and the knowing that comes from a higher consciousness, who is bringing you the message and what is its relevance to your life experiences at the moment. It's about learning the language of daydreams.

How can you advance your daydreaming skills?

- DEVELOP your daydreaming skills through meditation and relaxation. Set up your dream space and your dreamscape, embrace meditation as part of your daily life and remember to focus on your breath whenever you need a quiet moment.

- RECOGNIZE when you have slipped into a daydream. Take advantage of quiet times that foster daydreaming and catch yourself when you do. The more you do, the easier it will be to go back into your daydream or to daydream at will.

- FOCUS on the details. One detail usually leads to the next. If you can't recall, close your eyes, ask for a message, and then remember what comes to you.

- OBSERVE how each of your senses was affected. Daydreams are very sensory and can evoke scents, bodily sensations, sounds, images, feelings and memories. Did it make you happy, excited, fearful or nostalgic? The possibilities are endless and unique.

- WRITE IT OR RECORD IT. This is a wonderful tool in helping you piece together the overall picture. Sometimes messages in daydreams can be very subtle, and the act of writing or listening can unlock the secrets within. It is also important to note what you were thinking of, or doing when it happened, and what your mood was.

If you want to fully integrate all of these ideas, then by all means, start with meditation and create your dreamscape. You can take it with you wherever you go, no baggage ticket needed. It will always be at your beck and call. You don't have to rent it, buy it, or mortgage it, and you can refurbish or rearrange it anytime you like. All you have to do is close your eyes and relax to begin listening to the language of daydreams.

Chapter 18

THE CHAKRAS

Let us be silent, that we may hear the whispers of the gods.
~ Ralph Waldo Emerson

There are many facets to God's energy existing in the higher dimensions that we call Angels, guides and souls, and probably many more we have not yet named that act as messengers. After we learn, through meditation, to be still and aware, daydreams become their entryway. These envoys send a spark of energy that travels down from their higher vibrational levels and enters our energetic system through centers called the chakras. There, it manifests as a daydream, sometimes connecting to the body with a mild jolt. That is why when you come out of a daydream it feels so real, so physical and sometimes startling. Daydreams are their energetic delivery system.

Our energy field does not end with our body. There is a constant flow emanating several feet out from our physical form that interacts with and is affected by a universal energy field permeating everything around us. The energy from this field is carried through pathways, called meridians, to energy centers in our body known as chakras, an ancient Sanskrit word meaning spinning wheel.

It is generally believed there are seven major chakras, each one corresponding to a specific area of the body. They run in a channel aligned with the spine, beginning at its base and ascending to the top of the head, where we receive, assimilate and radiate energy to our glandular system, which in turn delivers energy to our organs.

Each of the seven major chakras corresponds with the color progression of the visible light spectrum—think rainbow— from red to purple. When you see color, you really perceive a frequency or oscillation, a waveform that is a vibration of light. Each color, starting with red oscillating the slowest, has a vibratory rate that increases as it progresses through the visible light spectrum, with purple oscillating the fastest. When our energy is as it should be we emanate a field of color.

There are also many minor chakras, but this is meant to be an *introduction* to learning about the chakras and how they function. You may investigate further as you go along in your own process.

From the front, the chakras are perceived as spinning discs, a small distance out from the physical body, expanding and shrinking to channel the flow of energy into, through and out of the body. From a side view they would appear to be funnel shaped, looking like mini-tornado plumes. The ancients sometimes depicted the chakras as a lotus flower, with each energetic center having more petals then the one before it.

Since we are primarily energy and are constantly bombarded with universal energy, the chakras are the key to balancing our energetic system. Think of this: if you plugged a light bulb into a huge amount of current, it would explode. So you need to transform that energy, or step it down to just the right amount of current to light the bulb without destroying it. Conversely, if there wasn't enough energy coming through the circuit, then the bulb wouldn't light. In that case, you would need to pull in more energy.

The chakras are energy modifiers that act as portals to direct the course of this energy and help us to process and transform it, raising or lowering our vibrations until they resonate in perfect harmony throughout the body.

Opening and aligning each chakra moves the energy through the body and out into the multi layers of the ethereal body, the field of energy surrounding the physical body, where it interacts with the universal field and everything we come in contact with. The clearer the field of energy, the easier it is to receive the messages and guidance that are sent to us via daydreams.

The three lower chakras are connected to physical and emotional energy, the three upper chakras with spiritual and mental energy. When they merge in the middle, the heart center, feelings are manifested.

As energy rises through each of the chakras, just like the light spectrum, its vibratory rate increases. Beginning with the area at the base of the spine, the first energy center is called the Root Chakra. It vibrates with the color red. To visualize this, imagine a spinning disc of red light extending in a funnel downward, pointing toward the earth, from the base of the spine. This chakra spins the slowest and is the point of entry for energy into the body. The root chakra is about life energy, and is what grounds us, connecting us to our bodies, the Earth and our physical survival. We are spiritual and energetic beings, but we are also physical and need to be grounded to be able to manifest in the physical world. This chakra is the seat of birth and affects our deepest sense of confidence, trust, safety and security. When balanced you feel comfortable in your own skin, trust yourself and are able to overcome challenges with both feet on the ground.

When out of alignment, this chakra closes down, stopping the flow of energy to the rest of the chakras, bringing insecurity, leaving you feeling fearful or anxious with no clear sense of purpose, or feeling so "flighty" that nothing gets accomplished and you feel like you're running around in circles.

The second center is the Sacral Chakra. It is located in the lower abdomen, or spleen area, just below your navel. It vibrates with the color orange. Imagine a spinning disc of orange light, moving a little faster then the previous one. This chakra brings in the energy of procreation, magnetic attraction, creativity and sexuality, and all the emotions therein. When in balance, it allows for artistic expression and passion for life, sensuality and reproduction. It is the center where we begin to use our physical energy to express ourselves and to create life.

When unbalanced, it leads to physical and sexual addictions, to feeling "stuck" in the physical world, unable to connect with a higher sense of purpose and blocks you from expressing yourself creatively.

The third center, known as the Solar Plexus Chakra, is located just above your navel. It vibrates with the color yellow. Imagine a spinning disc of yellow light in front of your diaphragm. It balances movement, the fight or flight response, and is the center of personal power and intention. It is the seat of physical intuition, evident when you feel things "in your gut." When in balance, it brings in tranquility and helps you deal with emotions in a calm and harmonious way. You feel strong and courageous and can handle your life experiences.

When unbalanced, you are either extremely fearful, wanting to run away from every situation and controlled by your emotions, or conversely, you have an overwhelming need to be very controlling and overpowering. Have you ever heard the term, "yellow-bellied coward"? Many of these well-known phrases originated with the chakras.

The fourth center is the Heart Chakra. It is the middle chakra; the bridge between the lower, physical and emotional centers, and the higher, spiritual and mental chakras. It is the center for devotion, love and forgiveness and it vibrates with the color green. It is where you learn your true identity, and your capacity for self love is defined. It allows you to send and receive love and open up to the higher dimensions. It brings in the energy of purity and allows you to find love in everything. When your heart center is open, you experience joy and fulfillment. A balanced heart chakra sends out a vibration of serene, inner peace. It is all about healing and love: love for the Divine, loving and nurturing yourself and others, and listening to the wisdom that comes from the heart, rather than the mind.

But if it is too open, without boundaries, you give with excess, trying to please everyone, leaving no room to receive, opening yourself up to disappointment, betrayal or heartbreak. If it is closed down, you can become cold, empty, unforgiving, or worse: cruel, jealous and envious, hence the saying, "green with envy.

The fifth chakra, the Throat Chakra, is the center for communication and expression. It is the bridge between the heart and the mind, the place where your innermost thoughts and feelings are expressed. The color vibration for the throat chakra is blue. This center is where you speak your truth, to yourself and others. The voice is the essence of sound, a vibration that can put words to loving emotions through speech and song, that soothes, educates and uplifts. Your sensory and emotional memories are tied to sound. When aligned, you are able to communicate fluently, whatever your mode of expression. You express rather then repress your thoughts and emotions, and you sing for pure joy without caring if you are on key. Many poets and singers have strong, balanced throat chakras.

When out of alignment, you choke back your words and keep everything bottled up inside. When people say, "I'm feeling so blue" it's because their throat chakra is blocked and they can't articulate what they feel. You become introverted and reclusive. The energy is blocked from flowing freely on your breath and can result in chronic sore throats. Or conversely, you can become outspoken, a "big mouth", who is verbally abusive and uses words as weapons.

The sixth chakra is the Brow Chakra and is located on the forehead between the eyebrows. It is also known as the third eye. It is the seat of psychic energy and heavenly spirituality. It enables you to be intuitive, visualize inspiration and conceptualize imaginative thoughts. It is the "place" of meditation, self-realization and where you manifest consciousness. When you daydream, images are brought into your mind through the third eye chakra. The color it vibrates with is indigo. Imagine a rapidly spinning disc the color of the deepest twilight sky, where the colors of dark blue and deep purple merge to form a perfect backdrop for the stars. This is the color of the infinite, where you begin to disconnect with the physical and connect with a higher consciousness. When balanced, you are self-aware and intuitive, clairvoyant and more concerned with the inner self than the outer self.

When closed down, you become overly analytical and logical, thinking, never feeling, and shut off to your intuition and the guidance that comes from the higher dimensions.

The seventh chakra is called the Crown Chakra. It is the fastest spinning chakra, located just above the top of your head, radiating upward. It vibrates with the color purple, which has always been associated with heads of state and church. This chakra is the connection to the Divine, to God energy. It takes you out of the physical plane and is the essence of your spiritual being, awakening you to the divinity within. It connects you with universal energy and the higher vibrations of Angels and souls. It uplifts your spirit and awakens consciousness. When in balance, it takes you out of yourself and you act for the highest good. You hold high ideals and are able to see truth beyond earthly spirituality. You feel a universal existence beyond a physical one, and can look beyond life to immortality and see yourself as a reflection of God.

When out of balance you become high-minded and "holier then thou." You justify your actions with ideals that are at the expense of others. You preach spirituality but threaten or punish to achieve your goals. Or you become so closed down that you cannot accept any idea of a higher consciousness. You cannot acknowledge any wisdom or guidance that is not rooted on the physical plane.

There is also a minor chakra that I like to recognize which is just above each ear. I perceive these chakras as small spinning discs of pink light, bringing in the energy of clairaudience, or psychic hearing. I work with the energy of these chakras when I do readings as it helps me to "hear" the messages from the other side.

To grasp the big picture of all the chakras working in harmony, imagine energy entering through the first chakra at the base of your spine, spinning slowly, and as it radiates up through your body, each time it reaches another chakra it spins a little bit faster, pulling in and emanating energy, each one vibrating to a color of the rainbow, finally moving to the top of your head and emerging through your crown center. At first you begin feeling this very subtly, like a tingling sensation as you focus on your body and each chakra center, and in time, more powerfully, as you literally feel your energy gain momentum, rising through the channel of the chakras and vibrating with a frequency that feels "other worldly." Your energy transcends the heavy density of the physical body and merges with a field of higher consciousness; the spiritual dimensions where the energy of Angels and souls reside, and ultimately with the Divine source.

By understanding these centers, you begin to understand how you can maintain a balanced energetic system. *Focus and intention* is the way to achieve that. Although the chakras function automatically, like breathing, they are affected by all the energy you encounter. By practicing the Chakra Meditation that I present in the next chapter, focusing on each chakra, intuitively visualizing it to be the perfect size, color and rotating at the perfect speed to process just the right amount of energy, you can create the necessary shift to keep them aligned and functioning at their optimal level.

I know for some of you reading this who has never heard of the chakras, this whole concept may seem indefinable. But think about this: you know how you can be going along, feeling fine, and all of a sudden you come into close contact with someone whose energy feels really negative and your mood quickly changes, leaving you feeling drained, depressed or very guarded? That is because human beings are designed to have a high vibration and when you encounter an energy field that has a low vibration you can be affected by it. So it's important to keep your energy field strong and clear.

Also, physical, mental or even emotional trauma can cause a chakra to close down, setting up blocks, causing an undercharged energy field resulting in discomfort or disease. Contrarily, if you are too open a chakra can become overcharged, flooding with energy. This can have the same negative effect on your physical body, where it can manifest as excessive fearfulness. It may seem like a good thing to be really open, and the more open your chakras are, the more psychic you will become. But that's not how it works. A healthy balance is the key. Bringing the chakras into balance and alignment has a distinct vibration that uplifts and energizes you as it brings in healing. You will instinctively open to the higher dimensions where you can safely pick up psychic messages, daydream and receive inspiration, while protecting yourself against negativity. You will be a walking vibration of light!

Chapter 19

CHAKRA MEDITATION

In the attitude of silence the soul finds the path in a clearer light, and what is elusive and deceptive resolves itself into crystal clearness.

~ Mahatma Gandhi

The ancients considered the Earth to be a living conduit irrigated by currents, or grids of energy. They aspired to control these energies, to harness and direct them in order to raise their own vibrations and connect with the Divine source of universal energy. By learning to "feel" these centers and work toward balancing them, you move energy up from the earth and let it flow between your "outer" and your "inner" self. When you achieve this, your energy is balanced and aligned. You are more open and receptive, and you just feel so alive. Your energetic system can fully process information and messages transmitted through your daydreams.

The way you can begin to identify the inner awareness of the chakras, and intuitively restore balance and flow, is through a chakra meditation. While meditating, you can ask your Angels and guides to show you what areas need help, or to send acknowledgement through the chakras.

For instance, if you are being contacted by a loved one who has passed over, you might feel pangs in your heart chakra as you think of them, or see the color green in your mind's eye. If you are receiving inspiration from the Archangels, you might feel an ever-so-slight pressure in the top of your head, your crown chakra that comes in the form of a daydream, or when you close your eyes you see yourself being encompassed by a purple light. Premonitions from your guides might be accompanied by a feeling of openness or expansion in the middle of your forehead, your third eye chakra, to draw your attention there, or you'll suddenly feel out of your body and you have a sense of something about to happen. When you have a "gut reaction" in the pit of your stomach, your solar plexus chakra, your Angels are telling you to take heed with what you are about to do, or are thinking of doing. Or you might glimpse the color yellow when you close your eyes.

So wherever your attention is being drawn too, trust that your Angels and guides are taking it there, using the energy of the chakras to instruct and channel information.

The following is my Chakra Meditation. I include my love of crystals and minerals to enhance the imagery and colors of the chakra centers, and also because the vibrations resonating from crystals and minerals help bring energy into alignment. It is also important to understand that so much of this chakra work relies on intuitiveness, trust and faith. When you understand the concepts and begin to visualize the chakras in your mind's eye, you will trust that your intuition will direct the process, and you will grow to have faith that your Angels and guides are working for your highest good. It will happen naturally when you meditate, and eventually, with practice, you will see it all as you would a daydream.

Here is the meditation.

I begin by lighting a candle and taking three, deep cleansing breaths. I imagine a column of white light descending around me, enveloping me with love and protection while two Angelic beings stand as sentinels on either side. I am standing at the water's edge, surrounded by a circle of seven large crystals, each one a color of the chakras. They are beautifully translucent, with reflective facets that gleam in the sun and give off a shimmering radiance. I release any negativity and allow it to flow down my body and out through my feet into the ground where it is absorbed and neutralized by the Earth. I focus my attention on the root chakra at the base of my spine and inhale deeply as I imagine the red crystal beginning to resonate with a low humming sound as it lights from within with a luminous glow. The beautiful radiance of the red color permeates my chakra center, activating the energy of the slowly spinning, perfectly shaped disc of red light, expanding and contracting as it intuitively pulls in, processes and releases energy. I become conscious of the movement of energy there, grounding me with gentle warmth, connecting my energy to the Earth. I allow my intuition to guide me, and I feel safe, harmonious and balanced.

I take a deep breath. As I inhale, I feel the energy rise, pulling it up to the next chakra center, over my lower abdomen, creating a rhythm between the breath and the chakra as it speeds up and expands. Now the orange crystal begins to whir and radiate. It energizes the spinning chakra, infusing it with bright orange color, expanding and contracting until it is perfectly sized, freeing away any blocks as the spiraling movement of creative energy becomes strong and aligned.

I breathe deeply and pull the energy up to my solar plexus. The yellow crystal begins humming and radiating yellow light, infusing this chakra with whirling energy. It spins faster and expands as it fills this center with strength and courage, expelling any fear and negativity until I am comfortable and relaxed.

I inhale and feel the energy rise into my heart chakra. The green crystal pulses a radiant light as it opens my heart center, spiraling ever faster, pulling in pure, boundless love, expanding out on waves of green luminosity in an eternal exchange of love. My physical and spiritual energies merge and I am filled with endless gratitude.

On a breath I bring the energy up into my throat chakra as the blue crystal glows, reverberating with the essence of sound. The speeding energy opens my throat center, allowing my voice to move fluidly and freely. My throat chakra feels clear, balanced and unhindered, sending the energy higher and faster on a wave gaining momentum.

I breathe deeply, drawing the energy up into the center of my forehead. The crystal of deep indigo radiates light and illuminates the quickly spinning orb of the brow chakra as I feel my psychic center open to the infinity of space, seeing my energy spiraling to the stars and connecting my intuition to my soul.

Then with a deep, final breath, the whirling purple crystal emits an amethyst beam that catapults the spinning energy up through my crown chakra and beyond the top of my head, moving out of my body and the physical realm, bursting like a fountain showering me with white light. I am one with the essence of the Divine.

Through this practice, I am able to feel the rush of energy called kundalini—vital energy lying dormant at the base of the spine until it is activated—each time I meditate. It helps me to remain a clear channel so I can receive messages in daydreams, for myself and others as a psychic messenger. It is also a helpful tool for healing the body. When I or my children feel depleted, I look at the affected area and the chakra center connected to it and begin visualizing and meditating, working toward bringing in healing energy and balancing the chakras into alignment. We are, after all, souls in a human body, and we need all the help we can get.

So speak with your Angels and spirit guides to help you identify problems and bring in healing energy through your chakras. Ask them to inspire your daydreams and help you seek answers. All you have to do is ask and they will come. You may not get what you want, but you will always get what you need, and when you find, after meditation, that you've slipped away into a daydream, let it happen fully, let yourself become totally engaged. Then step back, take a breath and recall where your soul went and why. Examine what you saw, felt, tasted, heard, smelled or remembered that could impact your life in a positive way, to help you take action, make changes, or be inspired.

Conclusion

REVERIE

When ideas float in our mind without any reflection or regard of the understanding, it is that which the French call reverie, our language has scarce a name for it.

- John Locke

The Archangels say we have forgotten our ability to manifest exactly what our souls need to experience in this life. That it is this "remembering" that will create the surge of recognition needed to change the way we live and view our lives. Daydreams are the single most accessible tool to help us do this. Why do we take this gift for granted?

We are creators of our own lives. Our thoughts, through our energy, are converted into actions. We think, feel, believe and act. Our actions can become all-consuming, and instead of allowing our thoughts and actions to flow, we set up roadblocks and become mired in stress. When we reach the point of saturation, daydreams are our safety valve. They are a refreshing respite that takes us out of the moment. They relax and renew us. We have stepped away from our bodies and connected with our soul. That is where the truth lies. There is information there—a message, a loved one, a guide, something fleeting that, if we pay attention, will put us back on our soul's path and in that one moment we have manifested a new and different reality.

It is a generally accepted belief that daydreaming is unconsciously done. I do not believe this to be true. I believe that our soul knows exactly where it is going and why. We are all Divine Souls. This life is just a short trip, and daydreams are our way to stay connected. We may not know when we need it, but our souls do. Your Angels, your spirit guides, your loved ones and your soul have done their job to help you, and now it is time to listen.

So my question to you is this: will you take a moment to remember all of the beautiful, intricate details of where your soul has just traveled, and the messages it has brought back? Close your eyes, listen for those whispers, and

- TRUST that there are no random happenings here.
- BELIEVE that daydreams are part of a master plan to help direct you to your soul's purpose in life.
- ACT upon this inspiration; to whatever you see, hear or feel however insignificant it may seem.

How does your life look when you are living your daydreams? It is a life lived openly, full of possibilities and steeped in gratitude. Outer balance isn't always possible; it's the inner balance that matters. We are on the precipice of great spiritual change, and as human beings are seekers of truth, whether we journey to find it, or we stumble upon it. Daydreams are a compass to help guide us. It may seem easier to stay immersed in the life we have, one filled with distraction, than to venture out of our comfort zone to embrace something new. But when we stretch ourselves to face something fearful, or remain open to an idea that we can't seem to wrap our minds around, we begin a quest of searching for answers that will resonate with our soul. Like Dorothy in the "Wizard of Oz," who could have stayed put and wait to be rescued, but decided instead to explore where the yellow brick road took her, to find her own way back. And what she found is what we have yet to realize: that the answers we are seeking are already within us. We are born into this life, and we leave our true home behind. Our soul yearns for what is missing and looks to fill that longing. But you need look no further then your daydreams. The answers you need are there.

When you become aware of the messages coming through daydreams, you can begin to live a balanced life based on truth, the truth your soul is already aware of. So close your eyes and connect to that place within and let it fill your soul. Connect to your inner core of consciousness and when you do, you will be filled with such a pure vibration of energy you will feel God's grace touch you.

You won't find the answers outside of yourself. You will find them in your daydreams, a place where cosmic doors are opened. They are doorways filled with guidance, inspiration, acknowledgement and love. Embrace your power, and you can change the world, one daydream at a time.

Daydream Journal

Printed in the United States
212305BV00004B/12/P